KING OF AYODHYA

Impartial Analysis of Life of Shri RAM

notionpress.com

KING OF AYODHYA

Impartial Analysis of Life of Shri RAM

(Translation of "Ayodhya Ka Raja")
Writer - Anil Shrivastava
Translator - Yuvraj Shrivastava

ANIL SHRIVASTAVA

notionpress.com

Notion Press

5 Muthu Kalathy Street, Triplicane,

Chennai - 600 005

First Published by Notion Press 2014

ISBN: 978-93-84381-82-0

DEDICATION

Dedicated to Anxious & Youth

GRATITUDE

Author is perosanally obliged to the following persons / creations

1. Valmiki Ramayan
2. Shri Ramcharitmanas
3. Adhyatm Ramayan
4. Vashishth Ramayan
5. Agni Puran
6. Padma Puran
7. Manu Smiriti
8. Prachin Bharat Ka Itihas
   (Shri Vidyadhar Mahajan)
9. Shri Pushkar Bhatnagar
10. Prof. Subhash Kak
11. National Geographic Data Center, USA
12. Dr. Ramavtar Sharma

Anil Shrivastava
Writer
December 2013

PREFACE

Hindus always revered BHAGWAN Ram as seventh incarnation of bhagwan Vishnu and construed him as an ideal, obeying & practicing all rules and regulations as avowed in religion.

By the use of modern technology, birth of Lord Ram has been traced & established to 7000 years back.

Since then the legendry & charismatic personality, who was & is so popular and center of faith and worship among millions of people, is always reproached - by the blinkered followers, politicians, novice reserachers, sychophants in a manner which - not only hurts directly the sentiments of believers/ followersbut also refrains young generation from getting attracted towards the beauty and reality of Indian culture.

Incidents of recent past, where a renowned statesperson addressed to females in a meeting that Lord Ram is not a symbolic husband. To refute & as a matter of thought even Valmiki or Tulsidas or any other historian has ever claimed that Ram was a good husband.

I remember one more incident when a political party organized a procession abusing and insulting Ram's idol on dashhara festival. Their argument was that Ram attacked on south India and killed the king and the day is celebrated in north India, so they will reply in the same manner.

Modern youth remains in confusion between contradictory sayings and grand festivals related to Ram.looking to the above problem, I decided myself to analyse the life and character of shri Ram, impartially and to put-up before youth and interested persons in simple language. This is the moto of this first creation with many mistakes being first effort, for which, I sincerely apologized before the authorities and devotees.Original Hindi version is already available on the website ***www.hinduwiki.in.***

CONCEPT OF GOD

According to modern science, development of human being took place slowly slowly, such as homosapians, Neanderthal etc.after gradual development of brain, experience etc. when man started thinking, he saw and thought about the items existing before him. Such as air, land, cosmic bodies, fire, trees, snakes etc. In the very beginning, he started to worship all the items, which were essential for life or harmful for life.then he thought of some immortal and omnipotent power, which is the creator and cause of all the things. Thus god came into existence as supreme power, omni potent, omni present, omniscient, immortal who saves from all the crisis and fulfills all the desires.

Einstene also said in a reply to the question related to existence of god – "In my view, god is great rule encompassing the whole universe. According to my belief godly truth is ultimate truth. Continual search of ultimate truth is net object of science." Time to time, scientists claimed that the ultimate particle, responsible for creation of world, had been obtained. For example, at the time of invention of molecule, then at the time of finding Atom, then at the time of disintegeration of atom in to electron, protron, nutron etc. Recently after an experiment in an underground Lab, Scientists felt presence of a very small particle which was not visible even by very powerful Microscopes. They immediately declared that god particle was obtained,which was named higsboson. But it could not be clearly stated, how this particle could be the cause of creation of so many lively creatures in different designs,colours and different behavior in water, in sky or in land. Actually science is only peeping into truth from remote, through its theories, inventions, apparataus etc. in view of science, truth is god. Thus search of truth could be accepted as worship of god and science could be accepted as theist.

According to hindu religion, in the beginning, there was only darkness all around, only ultimate being having no quality, no form was existing called super Soul (Brahm). The super soul thought to be many as he was only one and alone (Ekoaham Bahusyami). He opted qualitative form (Dwe Vov Brahmano Rupe Murtam Chaiwamurtam Cha), thus ultimate man took birth in Water, who was called "Narayan" being slept in water. The Brahma was born from naval lotus of Narayan and creation of universe started.

Keeping in view, history, geography, mythology and folk tales of india, probably a group of Aryans came to Uttarakhand (India) from Tibet crossing Himalaya in the leadership of Vishnu. This thought is based on a story, described in a book "Badrinath Mahatmya" and discussions with the monks of Badrinath. Vishnu liked this charming and beautiful place very much and decided to settledown there, but he was informed that the area was under control of a brave warrior, who could not be defeated, but he was very innocent, then by using his brain, Vishnu acquired this place, Badrinath and Shiv shifted to Kedarnath. Interesting short story, described in this book tells-when Shiv and parvati were going to river Alaknanda to take bath, Vishnu laid down on the way in form of a child and crying loudly. Mother Parvati ran towards child, Shiv cautioned her, saying she would be in trouble, but Parvati lifted the child and put him in her house, then Shiv and Parvati proceeded to Alaknanda. on return they found the door of their house, closed. After knocking, door opened and Vishnu was found enthroned. When asked by Parvati, Vishnu made Parvati responsible for his settlement there, then Shiv and Parvati proceeded to Kedarnath, leaving behind Badrinath.

One witness of this incident, is Adi Kedar (initial) Temple situated on steps, going down to river Alaknanda from temple of Badrinath. Bhagwan Vishnu is supposed to be omnipotent personality. Possibly, the basis of this thought is the logic that Vishnu settled his group or tribe in a safe charming place which was also having hot water spring, curing many deceases. Therefore, he was presumed as god.

At the time of creation of religious literature, powerful living being, who saved or guided the Aryan, was accepted as incarnation of Vishnu. Ten incarnations out of twenty four described in purans are significant. 1-Matsyavatar (Fish), 2-Kurmavatar (Tortoise), 3-Varahavatar (Boar), 4-Narsinghavatar (Half Lion & half Man), 5-Vamanavatar (Dwarf), 6-ParshuRam, 7-Ram, 8-Krishna, 9-Buddha and 10-Kalki in future. It is a matter of great interest to see that development of life on earth is in the same sequence. According to science, life originated in water in the beginning, which is represented by Matsyavatar. then Kurmavatar, a small creature living in water as well as on earth. then Varahavatar, which is a strong and big mammal, semi-developed human is represented by Narsinghavatar (Half animal & half man).

Developed brain (wise man) is represented by Vamanavatar. Parshuram avatar represents a strong man with firm determination. Ram avatar is symbol of ideals and principles, a developed man/society having knowledge of politics, diplomacy is represented by Krishna avatar, peace and brotherhood is essential as told by ninth incarnation, Lord Buddha. Tenth incarnation i.e. Kalki is already representing Kalyug (Machine age).

Though there are many Shlokas in Valmiki Ramayan, declaring Ram as incarnation of god (Balkand 15-18, Again 76/17, 19 Ayodhyakand 1/7, Aranyakand 3/37, Sunderkand 25/27, 31, 51/38, Yuddhkand 59/110, 95/25, complete 111 and 117th Sarga), but many commentators presumed these sayings, interpolated. When Vibhishan aproched Ram for shelter, Ram put up many logics and examples as Sugreeva, lakshman and others were not in fevour. Finally Sugreeva said helplessly- "Oh, king of kings, there is no surprise in your statement because you are most powerful and always firm on the way of truth" (6/18/36). In the same way, when Hanuman described the qualities of Ram, he did not tell Ram as god, but the qualities described were godly qualities. But it is to be kept in mind that Ramayan was written, when Ram became king and king was accepted as part of god. From Ram's birth to death of Rawan, Ram was never identified as incarnation, otherwise context of forest abode or kidnapping of Sita would not have happened. In the same way, shooting of arrow from back of tree, friendship with Sugreev and Vibhishan are good examples of politics and diplomacy. As far as, matter of Ram being incarnation, now a day also, some Saints are worshiped as incarnation, such as Adi Shankaracharya, Sai Baba etc. In case of Sai Baba, actual photograph is also available. After elapse of time, eminent persons and Saints are accepted as incarnation of god. Hindu religion is so liberal, that great saints and eminent guides of society are accepted as incarnation of "Vishnu" the god, for example, founders of different religions such Rishabh deo and Buddha are accepted as incarnation of vishnu by hindus. I fully believe that if the tradition of writing of Purans would have been continued, Moses, Crist, Mohammad, Gandhi would have been recognized as incarnations of god. Here quoting one example of Vishnu Puran will serve the purpose. One worshipper asked bhagwan Vishnu, when he is ultimate soul, creator of this universe, how do many others worship different powers? Bhagwan Vishnu replied- "Whoever worships anything assuming it, as creator of universe, the worship reaches to me and worshiper gets its fruit." Exercising this, in society there will be no conflict between religions.

Assuming Ram, a god or incarnation of god, critics and opponents raise many issues. Personality and qualities of a great ancestor hide behind. Many act of Ram have been described as act (Lila) of god. Henceforth, we will discuss life and character of Ram impartially onwards. Life of Ram has been described in many Purans, Bhagwat etc. According to Father Camille Bulke (Belgian Missionary), there are 350 Ramayans available in different languages in India and south east Asea. Therefore, Valmiki Ramayan has been taken as base for this creation, because sage Valmiki is believed to be contemporary. However, many books, works of many persons and material available on Internat have been referred with my own thinkings to explain the subject.

GENEALOGY

Vedas and Purans are called Shruti (Hearing) and Smriti (Memoir), certainly there may be many incoherence. As these books were written after thousands of years of creation/ actual happenings, moreover these books were written by worshipers of a particular deity, so it may be prodeity. However, there is no other better way to know the history of that period, because that period is called Prehistoric, Prevadic, Vadic and post Vadic period. With the help of Archeological tests, the period has been divided into old stone age, neo stone age, bronze age, iron age etc., but thus you can't know about the kings, his relatives, his fights.For this purpose you will have to depend on mythological books.

According to the Agnipuran, Ram was suryavanshi. Marichi was son of Brahma, his son was Kashyap, who was married to Daksh's daughter Aditi, who gave birth to twelve sons, one of them was Vivaswan (Surya, sun). Manu was son of Vivaswan and Sangya, (daughter of Vishwakarma). Therefore, he was called Vaivaswat Manu. Vaivaswat

Manu had ten sons, namely 1-Ikshwaku, 2-Nabhag, 3-Dhrista, 4-Sharyati, 5-Narishyant, 6-Pranshu, 7-Nrig, 8-Dishta, 9-Karush, 10-Prishadh. He was also having one daughter "Ila", who was married to Budh, son of Chandra. Their son was Pururva, who founded Chandrawansha. Manu's family members were known as Manav or Manushya. Ikshvaku had a son, Vikukshi who was king of deities for some time, then Vikukshi to Kakusth, Kakusth to Suyodhan, and Suyodhan to Prithu. Prithu had a son, named Vishvarandhi, his son was Ayu, then Ayu to Yuvnashva. Yuvanashva had a son namely Shravant, who is mentioned as Shravast in Vishnu Puran, founder of Shravasti (Uttar Pradesh). Shravant to Brihadashwa, Brihadashwa to Kuvalashwa, who was famous as Dhundhumar, he had three sons-Dridhashwa, Danda and Kapil, then Dridhashwa to Haryashwa and Pramodak. Haryashwa to Nikumbha, Nikumbha to Sanhitashwa. Sanhitashwa had two sons, Akrishashwa and Ranashwa. Ranashwa to Yuvnashwa, Yuvnashwa to Mandhata. Mandhata had two sons, Purukutsa and Muchukunda. Purukutsa to Trasdasyu, Trasdasyu to Sudhnwa, Sudhanwa to Tridhanwa, Tridhanwa to Tarun, Tarun to Satyavarta, Satyavrata to Satyaratha, whose son was king Harishchandra. Harishchandra's son was Rohitashwa, Rohitashwa to Vrik, Vrik to Bahu. Bahu had a son called Sagar. When Sagar was in the womb, his mother was given poison. Sagar took birth with poison (Gar), that's why he was called Sagar (With poison). Sagar had two wives, Prabha and Bhanumati. Prabha became mother of 60000 sons, while Bhanumati had only one i.e. Asamanj. All the 60 thousand sons were burnt to ashes by sage Kapila when they insulted the sage, during search of horse. Asamanj continued to grow family tree. Asamanj to Anshuman, Anshuman to Dilip, Dilip to Bhagirath, then Bhagirath to Nabhag, Nabhag to Ambarish, Ambarish to Sindhudweep, Sindhudweep to Shrutayu, Shrutayu to Rituparna, Rituparna to Kalmashpad, Kalmashpad to Servakarma, Sarvakarma to Anaranya, Anaranya to Nighna is the chain. Nighna was father of Dilip, Dilip had a son Raghu, who was father of Aja. Aja was father of Dashrath, who had four sons, Ram, Bharat, Lakshman and Youngest Shatrughan. Ram had two sons, Luv and Kush. in Valmiki Ramayan this list has some difference. last i.e. 94th of this list was Brihadbal who participated in Mahabharat and was killed by Abhimanyu. Thus this family was called Ikshvaku vansh, Surya vansh and Raghuvansh.

BIRTH OF RAM

Ayodhyapuri was founded by Manu or his eldest son Ikshvaku according to Purans. Boundary walls of this town were unbreakable, so war (Yuddha) was not possible against this puri, that's why the town was named, Ayodhya.

King Dashrath was having three chief queens and about 350 queens as per customery, but he was having no son. Reaching to middle age, He was quite worried and discussed the matter with his family priest, sage Vashishth. According to his advice, sage Shringi was invited to perform Putresthi Yagya(fire worship for son). Sage Shringi was residing near origin of Mahanadi, today near Sihawa in Dhamtari district of Chhattisgarh state. According to Valmiki Ramayan, Shanta, daughter of king Rompad/ Lompad was married to sage Shringi, but according to Vashishtha Ramayan, Shanta was daughter of king Dashrath, who was adopted by king Rompad, king of Dakshin (South) Koshal, a friend of king Dashrath. Here it is interesting to know that Ram's mother Kaushalya was a princess of Dakshin Koshla, her village is said to be Chandkhuri in Arang block, 30km away from Raipur, capital of Chhattisgarh.

Sage Rishyashring or Shringi, son of sage Vibhandak completed the Putreshthi Yagya with king Dashrath and gave Prasad (Kheer - Sweet Rice cooked in Milk) to distribute among chief queens. King gave half of Kheer to Kaushalya, half of balance Kheer to Sumitra i.e. 1/4 of total and half of remaining to Kaikeyi i.e. 1/8, balance 1/8 Kheer was again given to Sumitra. In due course of time, four sons were born, Ram by Kaushalya, Bharat by Kaikeyi, Lakshman and Shatrughan by Sumitra.

Present Ramlala Temple is supposed to be the birth place of Ram. In 1527c.e., temple at this place was destroyed by Meer Baki, commander of Baber and a Mosque was builtup, called Babari Mosque. A case was filed in the court of British government, after first independence war in 1858c.e. Babar attacked India in 1525c.e. and the incident of temple destruction happened in 1527c.e. In 1858c.e., a case was filed in court. According to official documents, Muajjin of mosque told the court that courtyard of Mosque was used by hindus to worship the god since last several years. Up to 1940c.e., the mosque was also known as Masjid-e-Janamsthan. The judge passed an order in march 1886c.e. stating- "I visited the disputed area yesterday. It was very unfortunate to destroy a temple, but it is too late to decide any thing after a gap of 356 years." Archeological survey of India found proof of temple as a result of excavation there, but no proof of birth of Ram was found. The case is still undecided for want of solid proof from any side. So it is clear that the dispute can be resolved only by Muslim community. Hindus also should mind the informations available from religious books. According to Valmiki Ramayan, Ayodhya was deserted & uninhabited after Ram, . During 1st century b.c.e., king Vikramaditya of Ujjain reached banks of a river while onpilgrimage. There were few huts of monks and villagers, surrounded by forest. The king felt at peace there & on further enquiry, he was informed that the village was Ayodhya. He initiated & completed construction of various memorials in consultation with villagers.

There is varied dispute and differences between mythological books and modern history regarding year of birth of Ram. Few days back, an officer of Indian revenue service, along with his associate, used Planetarium software for this purpose. This software is used by NASA for launching rockets and satellites to other planets. He fed the planetary positionas described in Valmiki Ramayan during birth of Ram. Planetory position is described in Balkand (10th Sarga), the date comes to 10th January 5114b.c., which is matching with Valmiki Ramayan.

POSITION OF STARS AT RAMA'S BIRTH

CHILDHOOD AND MARRIAGE

King Dashrath got four sons from three queens. Ram was eldest, who was son of Kaushalya, then Bharat of Kaikeyi, at last Lakshman and Shatrughna of Sumitra. Palace and public celebrated a lot. King Dashrath distributed complimentary and suitable gifts to every body. On growing, all four boys were intelligent and were having all qualities of a prince. Among all, Ram was very brave, brilliant and dearest to all; he was expert in Elephant and Horse riding. They were always busy in practising Archery and attending their father (Balkand 18/26, 18/27).

All the four were liking and caring each one, but naturally, two elder ones were followed by one younger brother,each. Ram did not sleep and eat without Lakshman. whenever Ram went out on horse, Lakshman followed him on horse with Bow and arrow. Shatrughna was very dear to Bharat, and vice-versa in the same way (Balkand 18/31, 18/32). All four brothers were always busy in studying vedas, practising Archery and attending their father.

One day sage Vishwamitra came to the court of king Dashrath and demanded for Ram for few days to protect his Yagya from demons. Ram was so calm and quiet that king Dashrath always considered him an innocent boy. King Dashrath requested sage Vishwamitra to excuse Ram, as he had still not completed 16 years of age; he had no proficieny to fight demons (Balkand 20/02). He also requested that he (dashrath) would fight against demons along with his four tier army, he whined before sage but the sage did not yield to the request. He became angry, told to king that breaking of promise was not the tradition of Raghuvanshies, then sage Vashishtha convinced the king to keep his promise as sage Vishwamitra was religion himself manifestly, he was most powerful person, top in the list of experts in use of all the arms in the world, then following the advice of sage Vashishtha, king Dashrath agreed to send Ram, Lakshman also accompanied him. At a distance of one and half yojan (One yojan is equal to four kos or 13 km) from Ayodhya, sage Vishwamitra with Ram and Lakshman rinsed and sipped waterof Saryu river, then he teached sacred Verse (Mantra) of Bala and Atibala to Ram, he did not feel fatigue or fever due to effect of these mantras.

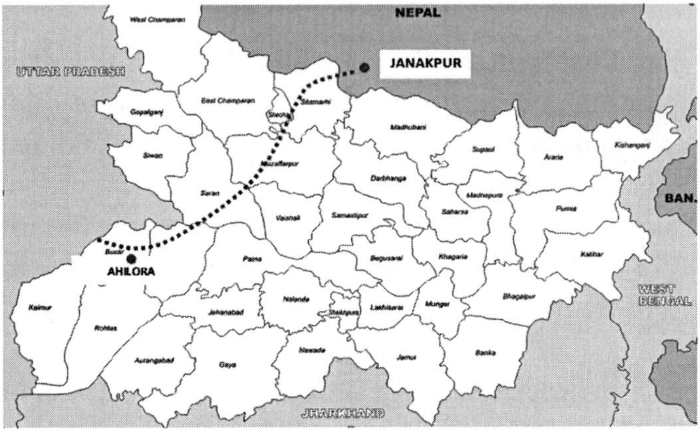

MAP NO. 01.

After attending the guru, both princes slept on a bed of grass and straw (Balkand 23/24). In the morning accompanying sage, Ram continued to enquire about all the spots on the way. Gradually they reached the confluence of Ganges and Saryu. After crossing the Ganges, they entered in to deep forest, which was called Tadka van, abode of Tadka, a demoness. There a hermitage was established by sage Vishwamitra, called Siddhashram. Tadka was obstructing religious rituals. When Tadka came face to face, she ran towards Ram to kill him, Ram said to Lakshman "he is not interested to slay her being female, so he should cut her hand and leg only", then sage Vishwamitra explained Ram not to leave her, as she was wicked and dangerous, moreover demons became unbeatable after evening. Therfore, she had to be killed before evening (Balkand 26/22). Accepting the advice, Ram showed his power of shooting the sound piercing arrow, he hedged her with arrows and shot a sharp arrow to tear her chest. They spent the night at the same place in the forest. Sage Vishwamitra was very pleased with the slaying of Tadka, he taught and provided many types of weapons to Ram. Sage Vishwamitra handed over a weapon, namely Nandan, favourite of Vidyadharas, and favourite of Gandharvas, Sammohan Astra. Prashaman Astra and Soumya Astra were also handed over to Ram. Durjanastra liked by Kamdeo, Manavastra favourite of Manavas, Maunastra of pishachas, were also handedover to Ram by sage Vishwamitra. More weapons, such as Tejprabh Astra of Surya (Sun), Shishirastra of Som (Moon), Darunastra of Twashta were also handedover to Ram. All these weapons obeyed the instructions of possessor. It was very difficult for deities also to possess such weapons. On return, Ram enquired about Siddhashram, where Vishnu practised penance during his Vaman incarnation. Reaching there, sage arranged to perform his desired religious Act (Yagya). Subahu and Marich, two sons of Tadka arrived there to obstruct him. Ram shot Shiteshu weapon on Marich, he was thrown away, on to sea shore. Subahu was killed by Agneyastra, used by Ram. Rest of demons was slayed by Vayvyastra. On performing the Yagya satisfactorily, sage said that he was obliged by Ram, he followed the instructions of Guru, fully. He praised him, that Ram was a glorious man, who realized the name of this Shelter (Balkand 30/36).

Next day, further programme was asked by Ram, sage intimated that he was invited in Yagya which had to be performed by king Janak of Janakpur. All of them, including disciples would accompany him. He also told that there was an extra ordinary Bow in the palace of Janak, Ram had to see it. This Bow was given to ancesters of Janak by lord Shiv. This Bow was worshiped as a deity in the palace.

Before reaching to Mithila, they arrived to an old shelter, which was located in a charming place, but life-less. Ram asked the sage, that it was looking like a hermitage but no monk was visible, why so? then the sage told him that, it was sage Gautam's hermitage. Where Sage Gautam used to live there with his wife Ahilya. One morning, when sage went to river to take bath, Indra reached, proposed to Ahilya- "Oh, beautiful lady, the years of youth are not to be wasted. I am very excitingly waiting for you." Ahilya accepted his proposal with curiosity (Balkand 38/19). When the storm was over, Ahilya said- "I am satisfied with this union. Now please go, before arrival of my husband and save me from his anger" (Balkand 38/20). As soon as, Indra departed, the sage arrived in wet clothes, understanding the situation, he cursed his wife to live alone in the hermitage, drowning in penance, eating air and roots of plants. Saying so, the sage left the shelter and Ahilya lived there alone. Sage Vishwamitra said– "Ram, you enter to the hermitage of sage Gautam and free Ahilya from curse". Then Ram entered in, with sage and brother Lakshman. He paid respect to Ahilya, she in return offered water and fruits to them. Ram also accepted this hospitality with great honour. Thus the lady abandoned by her husband, deserted by society, was freed from curse on arrival of Ram and went to her husband again. Ram's respect for ladies can be clearly seen from above two incidents.

Advancing ahead, sage Vishwamitra reached Mithila with Ram and Lakshman, in Yagya function of king Janak. After welcoming and greeting, king asked introduction of the two boys, then sage told their introduction, purpose of accompanying him, slaying of Tadka and Subahu and meeting with Ahilya etc. in detail. Lastly sage said that, they had come here to see the astonishing Bow. To know their introduction, Shatanand, priest of king Janak, felt thrilling, because he was son of sage Gautam and Ahilya, he asked- "Oh lord, my mother was in penance since last many years. Whether, she attended the guests." Sage Vishwamitra satisfied him saying that his mother met them and now she was living with his father, sage Gautam. When asked about the Bow, king Janak told that the Bow was entrusted to one of his ancestors, king Deorat.

King Janak decided that his adopted daughter Sita (who was found in a farm while ploughing) to marry a brave man, who could place string on the Bow. This was the Bow, in the hands of Shiva when he roared during Daksha's Yagya- "I will cut the throats of all the deities present here". Janaka's daughter was now reserved as fee for that bravery. He also told that, many kings asked hands of his daughter, but no body succeeded to pull and place the string, even no body could lift the Bow. On his refusal, all the kings assembled to marry Sita, attacked on him unitedly, then he faced and defeated them. If Ram could place the string on the Bow, he would happily perform the marriage of his daughter with Ram. Then king Dashrath instructed his secretaries to fetch the Bow. The Bow was brought in a box kept on 8 wheel trolly, pulled by several men. The Bow was worshipped and decorated with sandalwood and flowers. King Janak said–"This is the great Bow, which is always honoured and worshipped by kings of Mithila. Any Deity, Gandharva, Asura, demon, Nag, Yaksh or Kinnar could not lift this Bow, then, how can a man lift, place string on the Bow?"

Getting instruction from sage Vishwamitra, Ram lifted the Bow casually, holding in middle , placed the string bending down the Bow. Thousands of people were staring on that happening (Balkand 67/17). After placing string, as soon as, Rama stretched, it broke from middle and a thundering sound like a lightening stroke was heard. Every body there, was speechless for some time. In due course of time, king janak felt fit, and then he said that he had seen the bravery of Ram by his own eyes. Stretching, stringing and bending down Shiva's Bow was a strange, astonishing and unimaginable event.

His daughter Sita would spread the glory of Janak family, being wife of Ram. His words were fulfilled today; he would dedicate his daughter to Ram. Obtaining permission from sage Vishwamitra, king sent message through his ministers to Ayodhya, inviting king Dashrath for marriage of Ram and Sita.

King Dashrath also prepared as quickly as possible along with all queens, sons, secretaries, servants and army, a lot of silken clothes, ornaments, many decorated litters, elephants, horses for his daughter in law. He departed with those entire luggages to Mithila. In Mithila, after suitable welcoming and greetings, king Dashrath described his family tree, his ancesters. King Janak also folded his hands and described his genealogy like this- "In ancient times, king Nimi was a religious and best among all the brave and courageous men. His son was Mithi (On his name the area is called – Mithila). Mithi had one son, naming Janak, after him every king of the mithila was called "Janak" though each of them had a different name. List of descendants of Janak as follows- Udavasu from Janak, Nandivardhan from Udavasu, Suketu from Nandivardhan, then Deorat, son of Suketu, who was entrusted the Shiva's Bow. List continued as Brihadrath of Deorat, Mahavir of Brihadrath, Sudhriti of Mahavir, and Dhrishtketu of Sudhriti. Dhrishtketu's son was famous as Haryashwa. Then Maru was son of Haryashwa, Pratindhak of Maru, Kirtirath of Pratindhak, Deomidh of Kirtirath, Vibudh of Deomidh, then

Mahidhrak of Vibudh. Very powerful Kirtirat was son of Mahidhrak, then Maharoma of Kirtirat, Swarnroma of Maharoma, Hrswaroma of Swarnroma. King Hrswaroma had two sons, elder Seerdhwaj (He himself) and younger Kushdhwaj. His father enthroned him, his elder son and departed for forest abode. After some time, king Sudhanwa of Sankashya kingdom, attacked on Mithila. He sent a message through his ambassador to handover Sita and Shiva's Bow to him, but Janak fought and killed him in battle, then Seerdhwaj Janak enthroned his younger brother on Sankashya kingdom. He introduced his brother, king Kushdhwaj and then he described his will and offer to marry his daughters, Sita with Ram and Urmila with Lakshman. Thus, when king Janak committed, it was decided to start marriage rituals. Then sage Vishwamitra proposed, addressing king Janak that he had chosen the two beautiful daughters of king Kushdhwaj for Bharat and Shatrughan. He also suggested the king to offer all the four girls for marriage and to fasten the whole Ikshwaku family of Ayodhya in his relation. Then marriage of all four brothers with four sisters was finalized and rituals started. Ram was married with Sita, Bharat with Mandvi, Lakshman with Urmila and Shtrughna with Shrutkirti. It would be better to mention here that, Ram and Lakshman loved each other very much, in the same way Bharat and Shatrughan loved each other. In the same manner, marriages were performed, Ram and Lakshman were married to real sisters Sita and Urmila, Bharat and Shatrughan were married to real sisters Mandvi and Shrutkirti respectively. King Janak gave uncountable money, ornaments, cloths, horses, elephants etc. to sons-inlaw, daughters and guests on departure. Here I would like to mention, when Shri Ramavtar Sharma arrived Chhattisgarh for a lecture in relation to path used by Ram while going for forest abode, told that, some tax or rent was paid every year by Janakpur state to Ayodhya state for the land donated by king Janak in his daughter's marriages. This custom was stopped due to more expenditure, after independence and merger of states in India. Thus thousands of years old tradition was stopped due to money. According to description in Ramcharitmanas, sage Parshuram arrived when the Bow was broken, but in Valmiki Ramayan, it is narrated that Parshuram met Ram on the way when the barat was returning to Ayodhya. Every body saw that destroyer of prestige and dignity of kshatriya kings, son of sage Jamdagni of Bhrigu family was coming from front with an axe on his shoulder and a Bow in his hand. Looking at him, king and other army persons were frightened that he would kill kshatriyas again. Reaching closer, Parshuram said to Ram- "It is learnt that, your bravery is uncomparable. I heard Story of breaking of Shiv's Bow which is very astonishing and unimaginable. I have come here with another Bow, you place an arrow on it and show me your strength." Then depressed king Dashrath said to Parshuram- "You are now quiet, after showing your anger on kshatriyas, so please promise safety of my son". While King Dashrath was saying so, Parshuram neglected him & continued conversation with Ram- "There were two Bows, fabricated by Vishwakarma. One of them was given to Shiv to fight with Tripurasura, which has been broken by you, the other one was given to Vishnu, which is now in my hands, same strong and powerful.This Bow was entrusted to my ancesters. Now you place one arrow on the Bow, which can destroy enemy's fort or town. If you would succeed, I promise to award a chance of duel to you." (Balkand 75/27, 75/28).

Minding dignity of his father, Ram was not saying any thing, but on listening him, Ram said- "Bhargav (Descendent of Bhrigu), I am endowed with the traditions of kshatriyas (That is why, I am not saying any thing before a Brahman), but you are continuously scolding me. Now you see my strength and power". Saying thus, Ram took bow and arrow angrily from hands of Parshuram, placing arrow on it and keeping string stretched, Ram said to Parshuram- "Being brahman, you are honourable for me, moreover you are also related to sage Vishwamitra. Therefore, I could not shoot this killer arrow on your body. I destroy your quick moving power by this devine arrow, because this arrow can not be shot aimlessly". To witness that incident, members of each cast and society were present there. Then energyless Parshuram said slowly- "I never sleep on the earth during night, so was my vow to sage Kashyap. Therefore brave Raghav (descendent of Raghu), don't destroy this power. I will immediately proceed to Mahendra mountain. You destroy and aquire the areas, I have won till now. My inability revealed before you but I am not ashamed, because you are incarnation of Vishnu, who defeated me." After departure of Parshuram, Ram handed over the Bow to Varun. Knowing departure of Parshuram, king Dashrath became happy, he presumed that incident as his and his son Ram's rebirth, then marriage party proceeded towards Ayodhya.

AYODHYA INCIDENTS

When the marriage party reached Ayodhya, they found the town neat and clean, well decorated with flowers, streets were sprinkled with water, flags were waving on the top of every house. People of Ayodhya were waiting on entrance, with auspicious items in their hands to welcome the brides and bridegrooms. When the king entered the town, he, his sons and daughters- in- law were welcomed with Arti. Chief Queens Kaushalya, Sumitra, Kaikeyi with all queens became busy to alight their daughters-in-law from Palkies (Litter). Newly weded brides became busy in performing rituals, such as worship of deities, ceremonial salutation of father-inlaw and mothers-in–law. Afterwards all the four princes became busy in their married life happily. After some time, king Dashrath said to Bharat that his maternal uncle, Yudhajit was waiting for him to take him to his maternal grand father in Kaikeya Pradesh. Listening to these words of his father, Bharat thought of departure to Kaikeya Pradesh with his maternal uncle, Yudhajit.

Permission was granted by mothers, Shatrughna also accompanied him. During those days, journey was very troublesome and time taking, therefore stay at any place was also for long time.

Here, in Ayodhya, a series of incidents occurred. To understand these happenings correctly, one should know the working of kingdom of Ayodhya, as well as, character of Ram. For this purpose some shlokas are mentioned below-

"He always remained peaceful and spoke politely. If somebody speaks to him hard, he didn't reply". (Ayodhya Kand-01/10).

"If somebody showed kindness or supported him, he always remembered it. If somebody offended or exercised crime repeatedly, he used to forget it easily" (Ayodhya Kand-01/11).

"In between military manoeuvres, he always found time to talk to persons, who had more knowledge, senior to him and better in character and to learn from them" (Ayodhya Kand- 01/12).

"He always preferred and was devoted to his family traditions, towards kindness and to protect a refugee. He always signified his kshatriyaism. He assumed to achieve heaven following Kshatriya traditions "(Ayodhyakand- 01/16).

"He never tended towards evil and prohibited acts. He was never interested in hearing against religion and religious traditions. He always justified his side by arguing logically, like Brahaspati" (Ayodhyakand-01/17).

"Elder brother of Bharat, Ram was well trained in all the skills and arts. He was also having the knowledge of four Vedas including six genres. He was more skilled than his father in archery "(Ayodhyakand-01/20).

"He was well conversant with the essence of religion, economics and sex. He was brilliant and was having a good memory. He was capable of maintaining interest of common people and religion "(Ayodhyakand- 01/22).

"He was handling all type of weapons skillfully. He was expert in art of drama in Sanskrit and Prakrit language. He indulged himself in sex after religion and economics were over. He never opted for laziness" (Ayodhyakand- 01/27).

"He was expert in the use of musical instruments used for entertainment. He was having full knowledge of fund allotment. He was expert in riding and training the elephants and horses" (Ayodhyakand-01/28).

"He was best among all the experts in archery. Extra brave persons also admired him. He was deft in attacking and striking on enemies. He was expert in army operations" (Ayodhyakand-01/29).

From the above, it is clear that Ram was dearest to his father, popular in public and was having all good qualities. King Dashrath was now worried about his old age. Earlier it is described, when sage Vishwamitra asked king Dashrath to send Ram with him, Dashrath opposed strongly as Ram was not grown up and king treated him as a child, but when Ram killed demons and saved the Yagya of sage Vishwamitra, then married to Sita after breaking Shiva's bow, also operated the bow given by Parshuram, then king Dashrath became fully acquainted with the qualities of Ram. He was also doubtful about the intentions of Kaikeyi and Bharat. Therefore, he thought of enthroning Ram while he (King Dashrath) was alive. (Ayodhyakand-01/36).

While thorough study of Valmiki Ramayan, one would come to know,that king Dashrath married with Kaushalya and Sumitra respectively, but didn't had a son.Then he met with the king of Kaikeya Pradesh, when he was on an expedition. Seeing Kaikeyi, he proposed to marry her, saying he had no son and son of Kaikeyi would be king of Ayodhya in future. He promised like that on enquiring by king of kaikeya Pradesh, but when Putreshti Yagya was performed and Prasad (Kheer) was distributed among the chief queens, it was obvious that king Dashrath never wanted the would be son of Kaikeyi as king of Ayodhya. He gave half of the Kheer to Kaushalya i.e. 4/8, then 3/8 to Sumitra and rest 1/8 to Kaikeyi. One reason of such an act, might be caste/family of Kaikeyi. Kaushalya was from Suryavanshi kshatriya family of South Koshal. Sumitra also belonged to a reputed family and caste, while Kaikeyi was from a low caste i.e. Mlechha. Due to above referred promise, neither king of Kaikeya Pradesh was invited nor king Janak was invited in such a grand celebration. He called upon all the subordinate kings, feudatories, noble men, ministers, priests in his court and addressed them- "You all are well aware that my ancesters and my self ruled this great kingdom protecting the public as my sons. Doing this duty, I have become old. Now I want to retire this body assailed by age. My eldest son, Ram is better than me, in all fields of life. Among all conquerors, he is as good as deoraj Indra considering power and bravery. Therefore, I propose the throne of crown prince for Ram." He said further- "If you find this proposal suitable and if I have thought in right direction, you allow me to do so, otherwise tell me other options." (Ayodhyakand-02/15).

From the above, it is also noted, though kings were sovereign but they had to seek permission or to accept the advice of committee comprising of all sections of kingdom. All the men present in the meeting, applauded in support of king. The king again asked the public- "I am ruling this kingdom religiously, then why do you want Ram as crown prince in my presence". The public replied- "Ram is best among descendants of Ikshwaku. He has a pleasant and attractive personality, he is truthful, having a zcal for truth, hc has cstablishcd thc rcligion and economy. Ram is quite virtuous, dedicated towards truthfulness, having high morals, calm and polite in speaking. Best brahmans, expert in religion and economics have trained him. Whenever he proceeds for a war against enemy, he never returns without victory." (Ayodhyakand-02/36).

Thus, every man, present there, praised and declared that Ram was suitable to become crown prince. Then king Dashrath announced "Ram would be enthroned next day early morning & everyone should start preparations". All ministers, Brahmans, every one became engaged in preparetions, because of less time left. King Dashrath asked his minister Sumantra, to call Ram quickly. On arrival of Ram, king said- "Now no other work is left except enthroning you. Therefore, you obey the instruction, whatever I issue." (Ayodhyakand-04/15).

Here king Dashrath shared his doubts about Kaikeyi and Bharat with Ram. According to astrologers, Mangal and Rahu had encircled king's birth planet. He had bad dreams whole night. On appearing such evil signs, it was supposed that the king would suffer misfortune, even he could die. The king said- "Therefore Raghunandan (Son of Raghu), before my heart is covered with delusion, you finish your enthronement. Moreover, mind is unstable". (Ayodhyakand-04/20). "Till, Bharat is out of town, your enthronement should be finished, as I feel."(Ayodhyakand- 04/25).

Further, the king said to Ram that his younger brother, Bharat is a monk, controller of his wordly wishes, follower of his elder brother, but there is no surety of heart. Heart of religious person also could be covered with greed and jealousy. Then, Ram agreed to obey the instructions of his father and went to his palace to tell Sita, what was happening. Not finding Sita there, he went to his mother's room. There he saw his mother, Kaushalya engaged in worshiping god for enthronement of his son. Sumitra and Lakshman reached there, hearing the news of enthronement. Sita was also called there. On Ram's arrival every body expressed his pleasure. Ram said to Lakshman-"Lakshman, you rule this kingdom, along with me. You are my second soul, you enjoy this kingly status."(Ayodhyakand-04/43).

From the above description, it is evident that king Dashrath was doubting some obstruction on arrival of Bharat, that's why, he wanted to finish the work of enthronement as early as possible. Kaushalya, Sita, Sumitra and Lakshman were very happy. Ram already said to Lakshman to rule the kingdom jointly. Here, in town, preparations were on full swing, but Kaikeyi was not aware of the news. Kaikeyi had a maid-servent, very close to her, accompanying her from Kaikeya Pradesh called "Manthara". She went on the rooftop for some work. She saw that streets of Ayodhya were being sprinkled, flowers scattered, flags flying, doors of temples and private houses were being painted with sandalwood and lime, sound of musical instruments was spreading.Looking at the preparations manthara surprised, then she saw the foster mother of Ram on neighbouring rooftop. She asked the reason of her happiness and all these preparetions. Then she was told about Ram's enthronement in the next morning. Manthara immediately stepped down and roused Kaikeyi. She incited the Kaikeyi- "When Ram will become king, Kaushalya will be queen mother, you will be her slave. she will take revenge of every insult done by you. behavior of Ram with Bharat in future is also not known. Being step brother, there may be risk of his life." Then Kaikeyi awarded Manthara some ornament for the good news and said that she didn't find any difference between Ram and Bharat. But Manthara threw the ornament and again incited the Kaikeyi. Ultimately, Kaikeyi was influenced by Manthara and asked for some wayout. Manthara said to Kaikeyi- "Bharat was sent to his maternal grand father's house, in young age. If he would have been here, due to father's love, he might have got half of the kingdom. Due to insistent asking by Bharat, Shatrughna also accompanied him; otherwise he would have tried some means. Lakshman is here, who always protects and supports Ram. Their brotherhood is famous in all the three lokas. However, you told me many times that, in Dandkarnya, during war between deities and Shambarasur, king Dashrath became unconscious and then you saved his life by driving the chariot to a remote place. There also, he was again injured, and then you shifted the chariot to some other place. King Dashrath was pleased and granted to fulfill two demands on request. Those two grants are in pending. Now, firstly you can ask to enthrone Bharat, secondly, exile in forest abode to Ram for fourteen years. When Ram will be in forest for fourteen years, Bharat will develop love and respect in the hearts of public for himself and will stabilize himself in the kingdom." (Ayodhyakand-09/31).

Queen Kaikeyi laid down on floor in Kop-bhawan (Anger show room). In the evening, after finishing his important work, king Dashrath went to Kaikeyi's palace to tell her about Ram's enthronement. He didn't find her there, that had not happened before. On asking, he was intimated that queen Kaikeyi was in Kop-bhawan. King Dashrath went there and found Kaikeyi laying on floor. He asked the reason for such a behavior. Kaikeyi reminded him regarding two grants. King Dashrath asked to demand any thing. Then Kaikeyi demanded, throne for Bharat and fourteen years of forest abode for Ram.king requested, But Kaikeyi didn't give-up her stubbornness, she was insistent. King Dashrath could not convince Kaikeyi and didn't dare to ask Ram to goto forest for fourteen years, then Kaikeyi said- "You always boast to be truthful and firm on your words, then why are you trying to digest these grants." (Ayodhyakand-13/03).

King Dashrath again tried to explain that enthronement of Ram was not declared in any desolate place. He requested for favour, so that his words would not be untrue and he would not be a target for joke. But she didn't agree and whole night elapsed in unpicking and reweaving.

Next morning, sweat songs were being sung with musical instruments to awaken the king. Every thing was stopped by the king, immediately. Sage Vashishtha reached there and asked Sumantra in the mob assembled, to intimate the king that every thing was ready. When Sumantra reached inside the palace, found the king alert. The king asked him to call Ram at once. Sumantra cameback with Ram, Ram found the king in distress. King Dashrath became silent, saying "Ram"once. Even after repeated asking, he didn't say any thing. Then Ram asked Kaikeyi whether any fault or sin had been done unknowingly by him, due to which, father was annoyed or he was suffering from illness. Was there any bad news related to Bharat or Shatrughan? when asked repeatedly, Kaikeyi said- "The king is neither annoyed with you, nor he is suffering from any illness. He has something in his heart, which he can not reveal due to risk of your dissatisfaction. He can not say any thing unpleasant for you, but to keep his promises, you must obey his words."

Kaikeyi further said- "if the words, said by the king are not in vain in your ears. Then I will tell you in detail. He will not say any thing, directly to you." (Ayodhyakand- 18/26).

Ram was sorrowful, hearing this. He said- "I am reproachful, how have you said like this for me? what is the work, which can not be done on his order? If he wishes, I can jump into burning fire, can eat strong poison and dive in to sea. Please tell me whatever the king wishes, I will fulfill it." Kaikeyi told about two grants promised by the king, and said that was the only matter, but king was unable to tell due to fear of separation.

Hearing this, Ram said- "Very well, as desired would be done. I will proceed to forest for fourteen years, wearing matted hairs and tatters in compliance to my father's words." (Ayodhyakand-19/02) .

Ram further said to Kaikeyi- "The king is my wellwisher, teacher and father. On his wish and order, I can do anything undoubtedly, but I am chagrined that the king didn't tell me himself about the enthronement of Bharat. Only by your saying, I can abandon this kingdom, Sita, my life and all property happily. Then, if king orders for some work, that too, desired by you, why will I not undertake to comply it? I immediately proceed to Dandakaranya for fourteen years".

Hearing this, Kaikeyi became pleased and said- "You are quite right. A messenger will go soon to call Bharat, but Ram,you are very much anxious to go to forest, hence don't delay. You must leave as early as possible, the king is ashamed and therefore he is not saying himself. Till you don't proceed to forest, he will not go for a bath or food." Listening these words from Kaikeyi, the king became unconscious saying- "Shame on you."

Here one Shloka (Verse) is mentioned which confirms Kaikeyi , being un arya- "Listening these fearsome words from unarya dear, Ram became unhappy and said that though the king himself had not said, but he would go to forest for fourteen years onher say only." (Ayodhyakand-19/23).

Before departure, Ram told everything to Lakshman. then Lakshman said- "Till no body knows about your forest abode, you takeover the control of state in your hands." (Ayodhyakand-21/08).

Lakshman even suggested to arrest or to kill the king if he was opposing them, taking Kaikeyi's side. He explained that a teacher should had also be punished if he was on a wrong course due to arrogance. King had no courage to handover the kingdom to Bharat , till he (Lakshman) was there.

Lakshman said- "My aged father, who is engrossed in Kaikeyi, gone back to childhood and is censured in public, will definitely be killed by me." Mother Kaushalya also, said to Ram that after listening the words of Lakshman, he could do whatever was justified. He wanted to leave her own mother for compliance of ill-will of his step mother. Then Ram said- "Mother, I Bow my head on your feet, but in past, many sons had performed wretched acts on their father's order. Such as, sage Kandu slew a Cow, Pershuram cut his mother's throat as desired by his father. In our family also, sons of our ancestor king sagar were killed following father's order. I can not disobey my father's words. Moreover Kaikeyi is also my mother, hence I am going to forest."

When Ram met Sita, he explained all the difficulties and risks in forest. He advised her to remain in palace and to serve the king and mother. Sita blamed Ram ,due to fear of separation- "If my father ever thought, as son in law, you are male by body only. By acts you are a female." (Ayodhya kand-30/3).

Further, she said if world said that Ram was short of bravery and valour, it would be quite troublesome for her. Even after explaining repeatedly, Sita denied to stay in Ayodhya and then Ram agreed to take her with him. Here stubborn nature of Sita is noticed. Then Ram along with Sita and Lakshman, went to king Dashrath to ask permission to depart towards forest after donating their every thing to Brahmans and poors. Hearing Ram's arrival, king called all his queens (Around 350) in his room. All of them started weeping and said that he (Ram) never treated them different than Kaushalya. He was careful about them, what would happen to them after departure of Ram? King Dashrath said- "I fall in delusion of grants to Kaikeyi. You arrest me and occupy the throne of Ayodhya." (Ayodhyakand-34/26).

Ram said, folded his hands- "O king, you continue to rule for next thousands of years or you can enthrone Bharat, but I will live in forest for fourteen years. You comply the grants awarded to Kaikeyi during deity-demon war and be truthful."

Thus, even after support from all, obeying the religion and traditions, Ram departed to forest with Sita and Lakshman, kicking away the throne of Ayodhya.

FOREST ABODE

When Ram departed to forest along with Sita and Lakshman on a chariot, he was accompanied by a large group of public of Ayodhya. Ram tried to convince them to go back, saying if they wanted his early comeback, then they should not follow him any more. Now Bharat was their king. He was well qualified and capable, he was better than him (Ram), that's why king decided to enthrone Bharat. But residents of Ayodhya were not ready to leave due to respect and affection. In the night, they halted on the banks of river tamsa. Just before dawn, Ram awoke Sita, Lakshman and Sumantra and said that residents of Ayodhya would not leave him. Therfore, before their awakening, they (Ram, Sita, Lakshman and Sumantra) should had left for forest. They proceeded towards deep forest by chariot. Up to daybreak, they were far away. But, the residents of various villages on the path, looking on them, cursed the king and Kaikeyi. Then they reached Shringverpur on the bank of Ganges, where king of Nishadas, Guha was ruling.

Ram embraced guha though he belonged to lower cast and was resident of forest reason, saying he was like his brother. When Guha offered various types of food, he politely refused. He said-"I need the things required for horses, among all these things. Our welcome and honour will be over by this only." (Aranyakand-51/45).

He also demanded milk of banyan tree. By applying it, his hairs would become matted. Presently, this place is about twety km from Allahabad, on the banks of Ganges in north. In the morning, Ram asked Nishadraj Guha to provide a boat to cross Ganges. Then he instructed Sumantra to go back and said that they would proceed into forest onwards on foot. He adviced, Sumantra to convince and to console king Dashrath, all mothers, especially Bharat. But Sumantra insisted to accompany Ram. Ram then explained that when Sumantra would return to Ayodhya, then only, Kaikeyi would believe that Ram had gone to forest. Otherwise she would not be satisfied and would doubt the king. Then Sumantra returned to Ayodhya and others crossed Ganges by boat.

Ram advised to Nishadraj Guha- "You should always be alert regarding army, treasury, fort and kingdom, because to protect kingdom is very difficult. Then Ram instructed Guha to go back. Crossing river Ganges, they reached to Sangam (Confluence) in Prayag (Allahabad). He met sage Bhardwaj there, asked him suitable place for forest abode. Sage suggested living there, but Ram said that the place was very near to Ayodhya. It might cause frequent visits of residents of Ayodhya, then the sage would be disturbed. Then sage bhardwaj suggested him Chitrakut, suitable for forest abode and far away from Ayodhya. The sage also told him that many sages and monks were there, busy in ascetic practices. Atmosphere of chitrakut was very calm and pure. Then Ram Sita and Lakshman, all the three proceeded towards Chitrakut in the direction told by sage Bhardwaj. Chitrakut is situated in banda district, at the border of Uttar Pradesh and Madhya Pradesh. During stay of Ram in Chitrakut, abode of sage Valmiki was there. Every body reached there and paid respect to sage. On his advice, Lakshman prepared Purnkutee (A hut prepared with leaves and bamboos), one for Ram and Sita, another for him (for Lakshman) and then performed scriptural worship of deities (Vastu puja) with available flowers and fruits and started living there.

In Ayodhya, king Dashrath expired. Bharat and Shatrughan returned from Kaikeya Pradesh and were informed all the happenings. Bharat became angry with his mother Kaikeyi. Shatrughan fetched manthara, caught by her hairs, hitting by foot. Bharat prohibited him saying, she was a woman. If she died, Ram would become angery and would stop talking with both of them. If he (Bharat) would not had scared of Ram's anger, he would had killed his mother. Then Bharat arranged and completed his father's funeral in religious way.

Then Bharat stopped oprepations in progress to welcome him as king. He asked all ministers to go to forest with him to bring Ram back. Bharat reached Chitrakut alongwith all three mothers, ministers and other courtiers. He requested to Ram to come back and to enjoy the throne, as this was his right, but Ram relpied that he was there due to his father's order and the throne was awarded to him (to Bharat), therefore both of them, should had followed their father's desire. Bharat, mothers and all courtiers argued in many different manners, but Ram was not ready to return. Even sage Jabali tried to convince him like an atheist that nothing was sure beyond life hence, he should had enjoyed the life and kingdom. Ram became annoyed and said- "Your advice looks like religious advice but actually it is against religion. If I accept it, then it will not be according to Vedas. If I will not follow the Vedas strictly, who will respect me? In that condition, I will be a disgressed and misconducting person."

He continued, if a vow was broken, by what means, would he able to go to heaven? He would become a dictator and the public would also be out of control .To follow the truth was the duty of a king. Then sage Jabali begged to forgive him. Sage Vashishtha also told Ram that sage Jabali was only trying to take him back to Ayodhya, otherwise he was also a religious man, follower of Vedas. When Ram was not convinced by any logic, Bharat laid down a golden Charan-paduka (Footwear) and asked Ram to put his feet into it. Then Bharat declared those shoes as king, till return of Ram. Bharat returned to Ayodhya, keeping those shoes on his head and continued residing in a hut in Nandigram, not far away from Ayodhya. He also wore matted hairs for next fourteen years.

On return of Bharat, Ram saw that holy men there, were restless. They were trying to shift some where else. They were also murmuring, pointing towards Ram. Ram asked the head of the holy men, whether he had done any mistake? The old man told that they were under the risk of demon's attack due to Ram. Khar, younger brother of Rawan, was living in that forest. He was very cruel, rude and man eater. Since Ram's arrival, the demons were teasing the monks regularly, they threw the items for worshiping and poured water into sacred fire of Yagya. Therefore, they were planning to abandon that place, before any accident. If Ram was thinking in the same way, he could join them. Ram thought that he met there with his mothers and Bharat. He didn't forget those memories. Moreover, the land became dirty due to dung of elephants and horses of Bharat's army. Therefore, he decided to move some where else.

From Chitrakuta, Ram went to abode of sage Atri. They met sage and his wife Sati (Totally devoted wife) Ansuiya. Sati Ansuiya advised Sita to serve her husband through out if his life whole heartedly, Ram, always and gave some ornaments as gift. Then Ram, Sita and Lakshman entered into deep forest, called "Dandakaranya". Ram killed many demons on request by sages, then they reached abode of sage Sharbhang. Then meeting and consulting many monks and sages, they reached - abode of sage Sutikshna. As advised by sage Sutikshna, they travelled in south direction, through Chhattisgarh and reached upto Bhadrachalam in Andhra Pradesh. They stayed at many places in Chhattisgarh, such as Surguja, Korba, Shabarinarayan, Rajim etc. Shabarinarayan is supposed to be the place where Ram ate wild berry, offered by Shabari, a tribal woman. But according to Valmiki Ramayan, Shabari was living in matang forest near Pampa Sarover, presently near hospet Railway Station in Karnataka. They spent about ten years in Dandakaranya and then they went back to sage Sutikshna. Ram showed his willingness to meet sage Agustya, the teacher of sage Sutikshna. Sage Sutikshna directed them towards abode of brother of sage Agustya, who further directed them to sage Agustya's abode. Sage Agustya taught Ram about operation of many powerful devine weapons, then they constructed huts in Panchwati, near Godavari river in the place called Jan-sthan, presently Nasik in Maharashtra and lived there for few months. He paid tribute to his father with water of Godavari. One day, demoness Shurpnakha arrived there. She told them that she was sister of Rawan, the great king of Lanka. She proposed to marry Ram. Ram sent her to Lakshman, saying his wife was already with him. Lakshman also rejected her saying, he was a servant on duty. Shurpnakha got annoyed and stepped forward to kill Sita. Ram asked Lakshman not to banter with demoness. Being female, it was not justified to kill her, in view of Ram. Therefore he advised Lakshman, just to cut her nose and ears. Then Lakshman cut her nose and ears by sword. Shurpanakha went to her brother, Khar, the rular of that area. Khar attacked alongwith Dushan and a big army. Ram slashed all of them. After slaying of Khar, Dushan with whole army, Shurpanakha went to Rawan, told all happenings. Hearing terrible news, Rawan planned and went to Panchwati with Marich. Seeing a golden dear, (actually Marich) Sita insisted stubbornly to fetch the dear. Ram asked Lakshman to protect Sita and went behind golden dear to fulfill Sita's demand. Marich (Golden dear) screemed while dying, calling Sita and Lakshman. Sita asked Lakshman to go and to help Ram, as he was in trouble. Lakshman consoled her, that all deities, demons, could not defeat Ram unitedly there was turmoil in that deep forest, caused by demons. It was quite possible, that there was no golden dear. It might be an illusion created by any demon. Moreover elder brother had made him responsible for her protection. Therefore, he would not go any where, leaving Sita alone. Then Sita insisted Lakshman and said harsh words- "You are greedy for me. That is why, you are not going to help Ram. I understand, you wish Ram in trouble. There is no love for Ram in your heart." (Aranyakand-45/7).

Even than, Lakshman refused to go after Ram, then Sita again said- "Unarya, cruel,destroyer of family, I recognize you very well. You want Ram in great danger that is why, you are talking like this."

Listening her harsh words, Lakshman said that he could not reply to her, because she was venerable to him. But he was doubtful whether; he would see her alright on return with Ram. Said so, Lakshman proceeded in search of Ram. Getting a chance to take revenge, Rawan, the king of Lanka arrived there in make-up of a monk, living in forest. He praised her very much and asked about her and her family. Sita welcomed Rawan, because he was dressed like a Brahman monk. She offered water and fruits to him. During those days, it was impossible to neglect a guest, dressed like a Brahman. Asked by Rawan, Sita told him that she enjoyed palace of Ayodhya during twelve years of married life. On starting of thirteenth year, king Dashrath decided to enthrone Ram as crown prince. But due to stubbornness of queen Kaikeyi, they had to come to forest. By then, my husband was above twentyfive years and she was about eighteen years old. Sita asked about Rawan, then Rawan told her that he was king of Lanka and had come to kidnap her. Rawan also said that she would get every thing in his palace, what Ram could not give. Sita abused Rawan and then she was kidnapped. On the way, an old man, called Jatayu, tried to stop him, but in vain and Jatayu was wounded seriously by Rawan. While returning, Ram said to Lakshman that he should not had left Sita alone, then Lakshman told about her behaviour. Ram said unpleasingly, that he had done a mistake. He knew very well, that Ram was capable of handling demons, eventhen he left Sita due to her harsh words. Ram was not satisfied with the act of Lakshman. Then they came to their huts, Sita was not found there. Ram wept due to tragic separation of Sita. Ram and Lakshman searched Sita everywhere and reached to Jatayu. Jatayu told them that Sita was kidnapped by Rawan, the king of Lanka. Obstructing Rawan, he was wounded and was dying. Ram performed funeral of Jatayu after his sad demise, and proceeded towards south as told by Jatayu. Going towards south direction, Ram killed demons Ayomukhi, Kabandh and many others. Dying Kabandh advised him to contact Sugreeva in Kiskindha as he was well acquainted with the geography of south. Then they met Shabari a tribal near Pampa sarover, who was waiting for them. She offered tasted berries and Ram enjoyed those berries while Lakshman was surprising seeing Ram, eating remnants. Just a little away, Rishyamook hills in Matang forest was situated, where in, Sugreeva alongwith his four advisors was living. Here Ram's knowledge of diplomacy is apparent. He was eager to meet Sugreeva as advised by demon Kabandh. He planned to help Sugreeva in getting throne of Kiskindha, so that he would be obliged and would be indulged in search of Sita, along with his army. He proceeded towards Rishyamook hills.

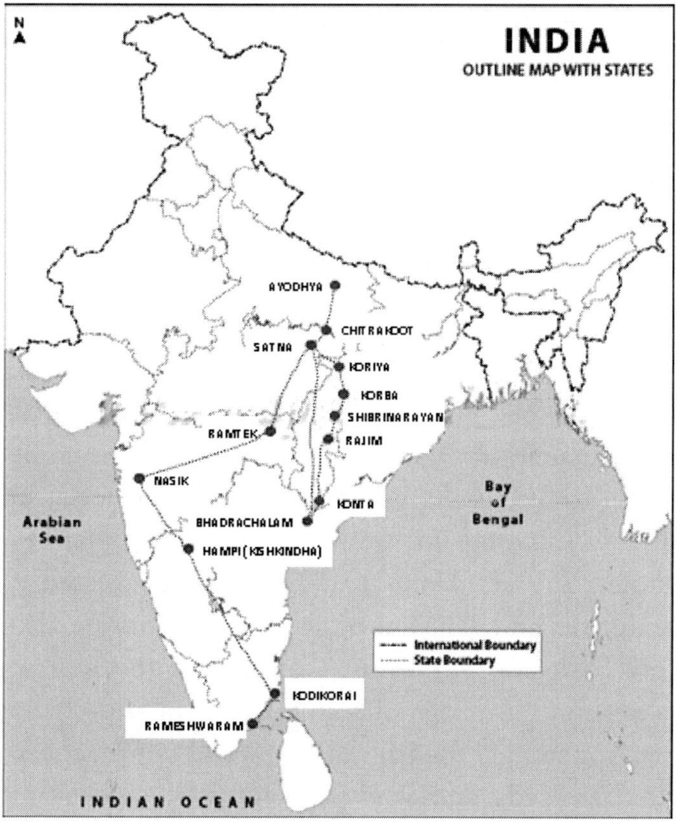

MAP NO. 02

KISHKINDHA EVENTS

When ever Ram use to weep because of tragic separation of Sita, Lakshman always consoled him and asked him to concentrate on search of Sita. Both reached Rishyamook hills. Sugreeva, on the top of the hill, was afraid of them. He thought that due to curse of sage Matang, Bali could not come there, so he might had sent his men in deceitful dress .Thinking so, Sugreeva sent Hanuman to enquire the fact. Hanuman went to them ,dressed as brahmana and asked about their intentions.he also told regarding Sugreeva. Considering the way of talking and language of Hanuman, Ram said- "who had not studied the Rigveda, who had not practiced the Yajurveda and who was not well conversant with the Samveda, could not speak so beautifully." (Kiskindhakand-3/28)

He also said- "certainly, he had studied whole grammar several times, because there was no mistake in his speech." (Kiskindhakand-3/29). Ram judged Hanuman fully by that short conversation. Hanuman also understood that Ram wanted to meet Sugreeva for some urgent work. Then Hanuman took them to Sugreeva for a meeting. There Ram told about kidnapping of Sita and Sugreeva told about his elder brother Bali. Hanuman made arrangements for their oath of friendship in presence of burning fire, then Sugreeva told Ram that, one day he saw a woman, captured and carried away by a demon. The woman might be Sita because she was crying in brittle voice- "ha Ram, ha Lakshman". He (Sugreeva) was on the ridge with all his ministers. Looking on them, the woman had dropped some beautiful ornaments. He fetched and showed the ornaments. Identifying those Sita's ornaments, Ram became very sad and asked the direction where Sita was taken, and then Ram promised to enthrone Sugreeva on Kiskindha kingdom. Sugreeva respectfully cautioned Ram about un-comparable strength of Bali. He used to up- root various types of trees. One demon named Dundubhi, was living there, he was very strong and huge. Bali killed him and threw his dead body far off by his foot. Sugreeva showed the skeleton of Dundubhi. Ram threw that heap by toe of his foot in one stroke. Sugreeva again said that it was skeleton only, while at the time Bali's incident, it was a heavy body with flesh and blood. Then Sugreeva took Ram to seven trees of Sal and told that all the leaves of each tree were dropped by shaking of Bali earliar. Also Bali pierced these trees one by one by arrow, if Ram could pierce any one tree, he (Sugreeva) would believe that Bali could be killed.

Ram shot an arrow towards all trees in one row- "the arrow shot by the brave man, pierced all the seven Sal trees and sank into earth deeply." (Kiskindhakand-12/3) Sugreeva was surprised and bowed his head on the feet of Ram. Then Sugreeva went to fight with Bali. During duel, Ram, who was behind a tree, could not kill Bali as he could not differentiate between Bali and Sugreeva due to similarity. Sugreeva came back, beaten badly. Ram told his problem to Sugreeva, then Sugreeva went again, wearing a garland and challenged Bali and then Ram, hiding himself behind a tree, shot one arrow by his bow and Bali was killed. Many curious persons raise a question here- why did Ram kill Bali, hiding behind a tree? Let us analyse the incident in detail.When Sugreeva challenged Bali second time and Bali was preparing himself to go for duel, Bali's wife Tara tried to convince him that just after beaten badly, challenging again, might be a conspiracy and had forbided him, but Bali said that he would not kill Sugreeva, but would teach a lesson. If Ram would had come from front, Bali might had killed Sugreeva or companions/assistants of Bali would had come forward in support of Bali, might had been killed by Ram along with Bali. In both cases, Ram was in loss.Because Ram needed Sugreeva with army of Kiskindha for search of Sita. Though in Valmiki Ramayan, Bali asked Ram why was he (Bali) killed by Ram while he had no enmity with Ram? He also said that he came there to fight with some one else, not with Ram, he was engaged in duel with some one. Further, Bali said that Ram had achieved disgrace only by killing him. He again said that he had come there, knowing the reputed family of Ram, though his wife forbided him. Ram replied- "you yourself don't know the religion, economics, sex rules and worldly customs, then why are you childishly criticizing me?" He further said- "this whole earth is under the reign of Ikshwaku family. Therefore, they are capable of punishing any body. We are wandering on earth to spreadout the religion, no body can behave against religion in the reign of king Bharat. Wife of younger brother was kept as wife by you. You have been punished due to this sin only. Sugreeva is now my friend and I have promised him to help in getting his wife and kingdom back. He has also promised me to help in search of Sita. Due to all these reasons, I had to punish you." (Kiskindhakand-18/4)

Bali apologies and requested for shelter for his wife Tara and son Angad. After death of Bali, Ram consoled Sugreeva and Angad and directed them for funeral of Bali according to Vadic rituals and to fulfill their duty. Then Ram insisted Sugreeva for his enthronement as king and to announce "Angad", the crown prince of Kiskindha. Ram refused to attend celebrations of enthronement as he could not enter a village or town during forest abode. While going back, Ram again cautioned Sugreeva that Shrawan (Rainy season) month had arrived, that was not the time for search or attack. Therefore he directed to Sugreeva to go to his town, they (Ram and Lakshman) would stay at the top of Rishyamook mountain. After rainy season, they would further go on to searching Sita.

Ram spent whole rainy season in grief, in memory of Sita. When rainy season passed away, Ram didn't see any action from Sugreeva. He thought that Sugreeva was fully indulged in sex. There was no news of Sita and time to attack on Rawan was passing away fast. Considering all those facts, Ram's heart was agitated. Consoled repeatedly by Lakshman, Ram stabilized himself and directed to Lakshman to go to Kiskindha to advise Sugreeva. Ram explained to Lakshman, how and what should be told - "who don't help their friends, don't accomplish friend's works, after fulfillment of their self desire, even flesh of such disloyal persons is not eaten by meat-eating animals." (Kiskindhakand-30/80)

"Path on which, Bali had gone, is still not closed. Therefore, you keep your promise, don't follow the path of Bali." (Kiskindhakand-30/81)

"Bali alone was killed by my arrow in battle-field, but if you deviate from the path of truth, you will be killed along with all your relatives and friends." (Kiskindhakand- 30/82)

Thus, Ram advising Lakshman, how to keep Sugreeva on right track, sent him to Kiskindha. Fearfull Sugreeva reached Ram and requested to forgive him, and then he deputed his messengers in all the directions to call Vanar (Monkey) group leaders, along with their armies. Then Ram said to Sugreeva consoling him- "o friend, I will defeat all the enemies in war with your help. You are my well-wisher and can help me."

Sugreeva deputed all the Vanars in all the directions, led by brave and experienced leaders and cautioned them to come back within one month with Sita's details. Probability of Sita's presence was much more in south direction. Therefore, he sent Hanuman, Angad, Jambwant etc. brave and intelligent assistants towards south. Ram also gave his own ring to Hanuman for recognition. When Hanuman went to south along with other monkeys, in search of Sita, they met Sampati, elder brother of Jatayu. They told Sampati about Jatayu's death. Sampati paid homage to Jatayu, and then told in detail about kidnapped Sita, about Lanka the residence of Rawan etc. Listening to this Hanuman crossed the sea and reached Lanka. There many incidents occurred, such as-meeting with Sita in Ashok Vatika, razing of Ashok Vatika, slaying of Akshaya Kumar, burning of Hanuman's tail and Lanka etc. While on way back, all of southern group enjoyed the fruits of Sugreeva's garden just before Kishkindha. Sugreeva was intimated about razing of his favourite garden. He understood that southern group enjoyed the fruits of his garden without fear of Sugreeva, while they were already late. It was clear that they were successful in their aim. Thats why they were behaving like that. Then Hanuman and all others arrived to Ram and Sugreeva. Jambvant told that Sita was in Lanka. Hanuman met her and now further he would tell you all the details.

Then Hanuman told Ram and others all the details of his journey, news of Sita. He also handedover Chudamani (ornament used to fasten hairs) of Sita to Ram as recognition. He told about Sita that she was deeply sad in restrictions of Rawan and had been very lean and thin. Rawan threatened her regularly. Ram praised Hanuman very much and said that the work done by Hanuman was impossible for Deities, Demons, Kinnaras, Gandharvas also. He was not only successful but returned, destroying Lanka. No body could be compared with Hanuman in bravery, courage and faith towards his master. Saying that, Ram embraced Hanuman, and then Ram asked every thing in detail- "you tell me, how many forts are there in that profound Lanka? I want to know all about Lanka in detail." (Yuddhkand-3/3) Then Hanuman described complete defence system, all departments of army, number of soldiers, number of horses, elephants and chariots, total population of Lanka, governance etc. He also told that Lanka was located on the top of Trikoot mountain, surrounded by sea. All around Lanka, deep trenches were there, which could not be crossed by boats? Lanka had been made safe with high walls all around. Ram was disappointed, hearing all those details. Then

Lakshman and Sugreeva encouraged him by saying if once they reached there, near Lanka, then Rawan was dead. Listening to thisRam enthusiastically ordered Sugreeva for march of his army towards Lanka. He also instructed that only young, strong and fit would join that march. Ram organized the mob in to an army efficiently.

"Commander Neel, you lead the army on such a path under trees quickly, where ample water, fruits and honey were available." (Yuddhkand-4/10)

"It is quite possible that demons may contaminate the fruits and water on the way. Therefore you must save these things carefully." (Yuddhkand-4/11)

Thus explained every risk, Ram and Lakshman sat on the shoulders of Hanuman and Angad, positioned in the center of army so they could keep an eye in all directions and army could also be encouraged.

LANKA-EVENTS

When army reached on the sea-shore, Ram instructed Sugreeva to divide the whole army into three divisions i.e. Vanaras (Monkey), Bhaloos (Bear) and Reechhas (Ape) to set them safely. Meanwhile, Vibhishan, youngest brother of Rawan, kicked away from Lanka, arrived there with his four ministers, asked for shelter, telling all happenings of Lanka. Ram discussed the matter with all his friends and advisors. Everybody was of the opinion that Vibhishan could not be relied upon, but Hanuman said that-"he can be relied upon because he has come for shelter. He has come, seeing cruelty of Rawan and Ram's bravery and for want of throne of Lanka. He will support Ram, will be in every body's interest. It will not be possible to check him or to depute detectives behind him, therefore, I feel that to accept Vibhishan's request will be justified." Ram became pleased, hearing his desired words from the mouth of Hanuman and said- "who has come to me in a friendly manner, I can not abandon him. Some defect is quite possible in the sheltered man, but saints have told not to refuse shelter for such person also." (Yuddhkand-18/3) After assurance of safety Vibhishan came to Ram, a bowed down on his feet and then Ram said to Vibhishan- "Vibhishan, you tell me the strength and loop holes of demons exactly and fully. Asked by Ram, Vibhishan started telling every thing." (Yuddhkand-19/7,8).

Listening every thing in detail from Vibhishan, Ram embraced him. Then he asked Lakshman to fetch some seawater and enthrone Vibhishan as king of Lanka, because he was eligible for that, he should had got that advantage. "Said so by Ram, Lakshman brought sea water and enthroned Vibhishan as king of Lanka in presense of all important vanaras." (Yuddhkand-19/26) That policy showed advantage immediately. Vibhishan recognized one detective, sent by Rawan. The detective told after beaten badly by Vanaras, asked by Ram, that he was sent to sow discord between Ram and Sugreeva. Ram instructed every body that detective was a messenger only, hence he had not to be beaten. Further, he would be kept arrested.

According to Valmiki Ramayan, as advised by Sugreeva and Vibhishan, Ram was on hunger-strike on sea shore. He was demanding a path from sea, to go to Lanka. But in my opinion, during three days, Ram surveyed sea shore from Kodikorai to Rameshwaram, along with his experts Nal and Neel, in search of suitable place for construction of bridge. However, the sea did not agree, Ram had threatened, it would be made dry, by shooting an arrow. Then sea appeared there, advised suitable place for construction of bridge. Whole army was engaged under the direction of Nal and Neel and bridge was ready in next five days.

Photograph of this bridge taken by NASA by satellite, is available on internet. As per practice, western culture has named it "ADAM'S BRIDGE" saying "RAMSETU" is non scientific and unbelievable to us, but it can be called Adam's Bridge. Which history, science or mythology says that Adam came there and constructed that bridge. That bridge was in dispute since long. Test results of stones used in the bridge tells that the stones are thousands and thousands of years old, when there was no life on earth, but the fact was forgotten that Ram had never erected a factory to produce stones. Vanaras used the stones lying around. Moreover, it is much surprising that length of the bridge is minimum distance between India and Srilanka. The sea is also shallow with full of natural rocks and it would had been easy to fill the gaps. Breaking of this bridge is under consideration since last few years. According to one wing, it is essential to break this bridge because presently to reach to Chennai (India), Ships have to take a round of Srilanka. After breaking this bridge, ships will reach straight, saving lot of money and time, but other wing says that this was constructed by Ram, hence it is a memorial of

Ram. Moreover, some technical question is there, as what will be the maximum capacity of the ship, which will move through, after the bridge is broken?

However every thing should be answered transparently.

However ,army of Ram, reached by side of Lanka, after construction of bridge. Then Ram ordered to release Rawan's detective as then he could not harm. Ram with Lakshman and Sugreeva went to the top of a hill nearby to spend the night. They saw Rawan, on the top of the roof of his palace. Seeing him, Sugreeva could not control himself and reached there, near Rawan, and then duel started between them. Then Sugreeva came back after some time. Ram embraced him, seeing many wounds on his body and said- "Sugreeva, you have shown this courage without my advice. Kings don't do such a dangerous act." (Yuddhkand- 41/2)

Next day Ram's army encircled Lanka. Troops on all the four entrences were posted. They stopped citizen, passing out and in. Ram again called all the heads to consult about further steps. It was decided in the meeting to send Angad to Rawan once again advising him for surrender. Ram sent a message to Rawan through Angad- "I am a ruler, who punishes the criminals. I am hurt, due to kidnapping of my wife by you. Therefore, I have come to Lanka on your door to punish you." (Yuddhkand-41/64)

"If you don't surrender with Sita, I will make this whole world without demons by my sharp arrows." (Yuddhkand-41/67)

Every thing understood very well, Angad went to Rawan's court and tried to convince him, but Rawan ordered his soldiers to catch and kill him. Angad skipped anyhow and started jumping on the roof top of Rawan's palace.

"With the strokes of his feet, the roof top of palace, cracked, just as, Himalayan peak was destroyed by lightening stroke in remote past." (Yuddhkand-42/18)

Roaring Angad returned back to Ram, then it was decided to invade Lanka.

The war stretched for many days. In the war, demons fought with various weapons and with divine powers. Vanaras fought with stones and tree branches. Vanar heads fought with Gada (Mace). Ram and Lakshman killed demons by arrows daily. The commanders of Rawan's army were slain one by one. When Meghnad, Rawan's son came into the battle field, he shot so many arrowes on the body of Ram and Lakshman, that there was no place left on their bodies without arrow. Their bodies were bleeding. All Vanara heads assembled around Ram and Lakshman, as their bodies were drenched with blood completely. Everybody became sad and distressed, and then Meghnad went back to

Lanka assuming Ram and Lakshman were dead and informed his father Rawan accordingly. Ram and Lakshman became fit with the treatment of Roots and Herbs and became ready to fight. During war in next few days, Rawan, Meghnad along with all his commanders and relatives were killed. In the war, Vibhishan with his assistants fought for Ram's side and killed many warriors of Rawan. After victory of Lanka, Vibhishan did funeral of Rawan and other relatives on advice of Ram. Though Vibhishan did not find it justified- "Who had abandoned the path of religion and justified activities, who was cruel, a lier and who touched other's wife, his funeral is not justified." (Yuddhkand-110/93)

Ram explained- "enmity continues till death. After death, it ends. Our goal is also achieved, now he is your brother as well as mine, so you perform his funeral according to his dignity." (Yuddhkand-110/100)

Ram instructed Lakshman to go to Lanka and to enthrone Vibhishan because he was his follower and wellwisher. He also desired to see Vibhishan as king of Lanka, then Lakshman enthroned Vibhishan on the kingdom of Lanka, and then Ram instructed Hanuman– "you enter Lanka after getting permission from king Vibhishan, then go to maithili and ask her welfare and health, intimate her all happenings and then come back." (112/24)

Accordingly Hanuman went to Ashok Vatika, wherein Sita was residing.he told all the news to Sita and came back with her message. Hanuman told Ram that Sita wanted to see him. Change in behavior of Ram is clearly visible from this point. Earliar, he was a deprived husband, who was crying for want of his wife and then was a conqueror. His behavior was in accordance to religion's directives and suitable for a king. He was behaving like that because he knew that he was under keen observation of public. He ordered Hanuman to fetch Sita after a bath and wearing good clothes and ornaments. Hanuman went towards women's section of king's palace and told to Sita accordingly. Sita prepared herself as desired, with beautiful make-up. Vibhishan fetched Sita in a royal litter covered with curtain. Ram was not happy with the arrival of Sita in a royal litter. There was mismanagement in the mob as every body was eager to look at Sita. Nobody was ready to disperse even after order, and then Ram stopped the dispersion of Vanaras. He said to Vibhishan- "house, clothes and walls can not become curtain for woman. Honour achieved from her husband and her good behavior is her curtain (114/27). therefore, Janki should come on foot upto me, so that everybody could see her." (114/30)

Vibhishan, Lakshman, Sugreeva and Hanuman were distressed because every action of Ram was hinting that he had become impartial towards Sita.

Sita was pleased to see Ram but Ram started to tell his intentions-

"O lady, I freed you from the claws of enemy, by defeating him in war. Whatever could be done by manliness, has been done by me." (115/2)

"To take revenge of my insult and to save my respect, I slew Rawan." (115/13)

"O blessed lady, you must know why I bore the load of war and got victory by bravery of my friends, is not only to get you." (115/15)

"To protect religious conduct, to demolish misconduct and to washout the blame on my reputed family, I have done all these." (115/16)

"Who will be the brilliant person from a noble family, who can accept the lady, lived in other person's house, only due to attraction that he lived with her for a long time." (115/19) "The purpose for which I won you, has been fulfilled. Blame on my family has been washed out. Now there is no attachment between us. Therefore, you are free to go any where you desire." (115/21)

"Site, Rawan could not had refrain himself for much time from your divine beauty in his own house." (115/24)

Sita felt hurt, felt pain in her heart listening those words overpowered by anger. She felt ashamed. She justified her purity through many logics and said that, she was not like as was presumed. She further said that she was helpless when she was kidnapped and touched by Rawan. Ram didn't mind her helplessness while kidnapping, then she instructed Lakshman to prepare a pyre, because she would not like to live a defamed life. She said that her lord had abandoned her in a public meeting openly. Therefore, in that condition, it was justified to enter in burning fire. Hinted by Ram, Lakshman prepared a pyre, then Sita went in front of fire, clubbing her fingers and said- "If my heart has not stayed away from Ram even for a second, then deity of fire, witness of whole world, may save me." (116/25)

Said so, Sita took a round of pyre and entered into fire without any hesitation. The mob, full of children and old men, saw the Sita entered into burning fire. Then deity of fire (Agnideo) appeared personally and said to Ram- "Ram, your wife Sita had no sin or mistake in her." (118/5) Then Ram said to deity of fire in reply- "to have faith by public in Sita's purity, this test was essential, because Sita had lived helplessly in Rawan's palace for a long period." (118/13)

"If I would not had tested Sita in front of public, people would have said that Ram was lustful and stupid." (118/14) "I didn't stop Sita, taking shelter of truth, so that all the three tiers of world could believe purity of Sita." (118/17) "Mithilesh Kumari Janki is sacred in this three tier world. A wise person can never leave his glory. In the same way, I can never abandon Sita." (118/20)

Saying so, Ram accepted Sita as his wife. Next morning after greeting each other, Ram said to Vibhishan that Bharat was suffering & waiting for him only. Without meeting him, he (Ram) was not enjoying any thing even bath. Therefore Vibhishan had to mind that they could return Ayodhya as fast as possible, because foot route to Ayodhya was very long & tough. Vibhishan told to Ram about Pushpak Viman (Aircraft), by using it, they could reach Ayodhya in a day. Then Vibhishan asked, what more he could had done for them, Ram said- "all these Vanaras had worked hard and took much risk in war. Therefore Vibhishan should honour them with gold and jewel by that act, everybody would known that Vibhishan don't only collect the wealth, but also distribut in justified manner". Ram advised about policies to Vibhishana and boarded on Pushpak with Sita and Lakshman. Then Vibhishan, Sugreeva, Hanuman all main persons insisted to go to Ayodhya with him. Ram accepted their request and all of them boarded on Pushpak. During journey, they halted at Kishkindha for one day, as Sita was willing to meet tara and others. While on journey by aircraft, Ram had shown all the spots, such as Pampa Sarover, Rishyamook mountain, Jansthan, hermitage of sages etc. Reached Bharadwaj's abode, Ram met with sage Bhardwaj. He was anxious to know about Bharat and about his mothers, therefore, he instructed to

Hanuman to go to Ayodhya fast, to intimate Bharat all the news that Ram was coming back, successful in his goal and with demon king Vibhishan, Sugreeva, Hanuman etc. and to come back immediately with all news. He also instructed hanuman to stop on the way at Shringverpur and to meet Nishadraj Guha. He again advised Hanuman-

"Carefully watch the reaction on the face of Bharat, listening my arrival and also try to understand Bharat's behavior about me." (125/14)

"Anybody can change his mind, if a kingdom, full of luxuries, elephants, horses, chariots and other property is available to him." (125/16)

"If due to company or due to self desire, Bharat wishes to rule himself, he can rule without any doubt." (125/17)

"Knowing Bharat's thought and his decision, you come back fast, till then we will be proceeding slowly." (125/18)

Hanuman met with Bharat in Nandigram(located near faizabad at a distance of about 12kms from ayodhya), where he was living since last fourteen years. Listening arrival of Ram, Bharat became pleased and sent Hanuman back immediately, to fetch Ram and others without delay.

Listening the news, preparations started on full swing in Ayodhya to welcome Ram, Sita and

Lakshman. when Pushpak arrived at Nandigram, residents of Ayodhya were present in great number with drums and other musical instruments.

After cutting of matted hairs and taking bath, a royal procession of Ram, Sita and Lakshman marched towards Ayodhya from Nandigram. In Ayodhya, Ram was enthroned according to royal traditions as king of Ayodhya. Then Ram-Rajya started where in, no body was in any trouble. Every where, there was reign of religion. The king had not to utilize his judicial powers. After few days, king Janak of Mithila, king Yudhajit of Kaikeya and all other kings and other noble persons, invited for enthronement of Ram, were sent off with full respect. Vibhishan, Sugreeva Hanuman and others were also sent off from Ayodhya. Ram had been buisy for whole day in administrative problems. In the evening, he took rest in his palace with Sita.

Actually, Valmiki Ramayan ends here only-

"In past, the epic created by Valmiki, is this only. He, who listenes this faithfully, overcomes a dire difficulty." (128/112)

RAM-RAJYA

Then chapter Uttarkand comes, which was added after lapse of long time, after Valmiki, because there are mythological stories, arrival of deities, reabandonment of Sita, slaying of Shambook, incorporated. Above stories were described in different ways in different languages in India and in South East Asea. in Ram-charit-manas Uttarkand, worshiping of Ram as incarnation is described. However, since Ram is always charged on the basis of Uttarkand of Valmiki Ramayan, it has to be discussed necessarily.

After a few months of Ram-Rajya (Reign of Ram), Sita intimated Ram regarding her pregnancy. Ram became pleased and asked her wishes, then Sita said that she wanted to go to hermitages of sages on the bank of ganges once again. She wanted to spend a night in hermitage. That was her only wish. Ram assured her that she would go there next morning.

In the night, Ram spent some time with his friends. names of these friends were-Vijay, Madhumatt, Kashyap, Mangal, Kul, Suraji, Kaliya,

Bhadra, Dantvaktra and Sumagata. These friends were not only gossiping, but were also informing actual condition of kingdom. Ram asked them, what was the hot topic in public in Ayodhya town as well as other parts of kingdom. "What are the good or bad talks in public about me? Tell me every thing completely, so that I can refrain myself from bad things they talk and follow the good things according to them." (Uttarkand-43/10)

Then Bhadra, clubbing his hands, told that Ram was praised for his bravery and strength. He also told that public was surprised that Ram had no doubt or anger about character of Sita.

"How does Ram feel in night, while meeting Sita. Rawan forcefully kidnapped her in his arms, then he took her to Lanka and there she was kept in Ashok Vatika, which was part of Rawan's Harem (Reserved area for queens). She was under control of Rawan for long period, even then Ram does not disgust with her. Now onwards, we will have to bear such behavior of our wives, because public follows their king." (Uttarkand-43/17,18,19)

Listening Bhadra's harsh words, Ram sadly asked rest of them whether the statement was correct. Everybody told bowing their heads towards earth, that there was no doubt in statement of Bhadra. sent off all, Ram called his brothers Bharat, Lakshman and Shatrughna and told them the situation. He said to Lakshman that he was well aware that how she was kidnapped by Rawan forcefully, then after victory of Lanka, he (Ram) had a doubt in his heart, how couldshe be taken to Ayodhya, after a long stay in Rawan's palace? then, Agnideo (Fire deity) himself appeared and confirmed her purity. His (Ram) soul also considered her purity that was when, she was permitted to come to Ayodhya.

"Now this censure is spreading all over. Everybody is pointing on me in the town. Therefore, I feel much hurt. Whose defamation is discussed by all, in this world, he goes to hell and remain there till his defamation." (45/12) "Brothers, I can abandon my soul and even you all, due to fear of defamation. Then abandonment of Sita, is nothing for me." (45/14)

Then Ram ordered Lakshman to take Sita to the forest near Ganges in the morning and to leave there, near sage Valmiki's hermitage. Ram also warned them not to resist and not to think more. He said, if they respected him, then they had to follow the order. Ram also told them that Sita wished to go to hermitages of sages and to spend a night there. Her wish had to be fulfilled. Next morning, Lakshman came to Sita to pick her in royal chariot. Sita took many clothes, jewellary for wives of sages and departed to forest with Lakshman. On Reaching banks of river Ganga where Valmiki's hermitage was located on the other bank(near bithur kanpur), Lakshman told to Sita that she was abandoned by Ram. Then Sita said so many things and also said

"From my side, you have to tell to Ram and you also see that I am pregnant now."

Lakshman left her there and returned to Ayodhya. Sita took shelter in sage Valmiki's hermitage. After due time, twins were born, named Kush and Luv.

Here, to discuss Sita's abandonment will not be out of subject. Ram already told earlier that, he could abandon any body including Sita, being cause of his defamation. Let us also observe the condition of woman in that period. Because, generally public and especially Ram, always followed the guidelines of religion. Manu smriti says-

"Woman is protected by father in her childhood, by husband in her youth and by son in her old age. Woman is never eligible for freedom." (9/3)

"Drinking alcohol, bad company, separation from husband, wandering here and there, sleeping untimely and living in other's house, these are six sins of woman." (9/13)

Modern historians also tell us that condition of women in Vadic age was not good. Kidnapping of woman was called 'Rakshas Vivah' (Demon's marriage) and kidnapper could retain the woman if her relatives were defeated. If a woman was raped, then she was also punished with the rapist. When Sahastrarjuna raped Renuka, then Parshuram cut his mother's throat by order of his father sage Jamdagni. In the same way, sage Gautam abandoned his wife. In Mahabharat age also, Draupadi was equally distributed among all Pandvas and was lost by Yudhishthira in gambling.

Question is asked that Ram was king, he could do anything according to his own will. No, it was not possible. Kings were not sovereign. They rule in line with the guidelines of religion and priests and according to advice of advisory committee. The king was actually head of state. He had to obey the directives of sages and priests (History by vidyadhar mahajan).

It is notable here, if any king started dictating, didn't follow directives of religion and priests, he was deposed by priests and Brahmans. When king Ven disliked performing rituals like Yagya, Hawan (Worshiping of deities through fire), he was slain and his son Prithu was enthroned by Brahmins.

Ram himself was a strict follower of religion and policies and guidelines of religious books, that was why he assumed better to abandon Sita. However, he never married again. Though during his period and afterwards, it was customary that, kings married many women. In addition to these wives, they kept many other women. In such an atmosphere, Ram abandoned Sita under the pressure of comman man & priests but was always sorry for her and hence never married again.

Meanwhile, about twelve years passed. Ram desired to perform Ashwamedha Yagya (Horse offering) in Namisharanya(at about 90Kms from lucknow towards sitapur) on the banks of river Gomati, --.. Sage Valmiki was invited and arrived with Kush and Luv. Kush and Luv sang Rama's story teached by sage Valmiki, moving all around. Then Ram came to know that Kush and Luv were his sons, as they were copy of childhood image of Ram. Ram sent Lakshman to fetch Sita but Sita refused. Then Lakshman was again sent, and became successful in bringing Sita to Namisharanya. Ram again asked her for fire test (Agnipariksha) in front of commen people.

"If Sita's character is pure and if there is no sin in her heart, then she ask permission from sage Valmiki and prove her purity in front of common people." (4)

Then Sita came before mob. Valmiki assured rama regarding purity of Sita and said that, she would take oath of her purity, but Ram says- "I have no doubt about Sita. I know that, Kush and Luv are my sons, but my favour and love is possible only when her purity is proved in front of public." (5)

Then, Sita on oath, requested mother earth if she (Sita) was pure, earth would place Sita in her lap. Then, earth cracked and Sita entered inside. Earth became leveled immediately. It will be important here to mention the description of Padma Purana. According to Padma Purana,

When Sita came to Namisharanya, after several requests made by Lakshman, Ram alongwith common people of Ayodhya welcomed Sita, appearing personally. Then, after bath, she wore decorative clothes and ornaments and completed the Yagya, sat on the side of Ram. After this incident, Ram and Sita lived long. One doubt rises here that, Sita sank into earth in Namisharanya, where the Yagya was being performed, but Sitamarhi, on the way to Varanasi from Allahabad, is identified as the place where Sita sank into earth (Map-3).

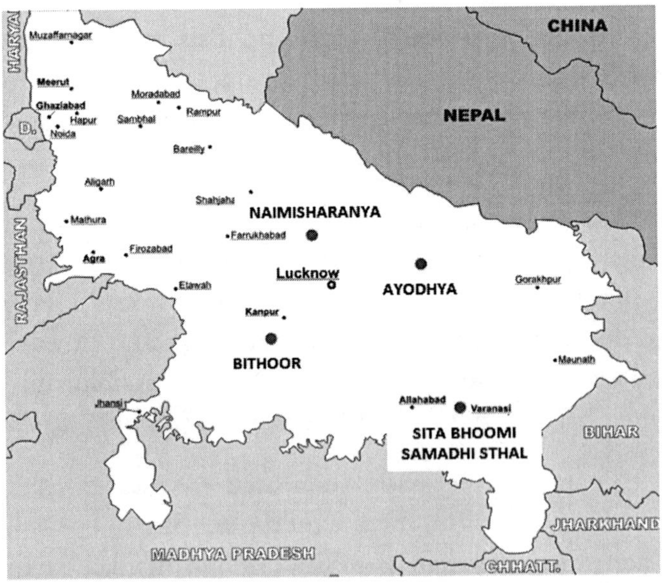

MAP NO. 03

Looking to the above, it is quite possible that Sita and Ram lived together for many years and afterwards while on pilgrimage, the accident might had occurred due to earthquake, which was incorporated in Ramayan later-on. There are proofs that Valmiki Ramayan was amended many times and few parts were incorporated. The words Buddha and Tathagata (Buddha) were used repeatedly for atheist. Ramayan age was much much before the time of Buddha.

Now we come to a horrible and most criticized happening i.e. Shambook vadh (Slaying of shambook). One day, an old brahamana came to palace gate, with dead body of his son in his hands. The boy was around fourteen years old. The Brahman was weeping and saying that he never told lie or hurted any living creature, then why was his son dead in his childhood? In the reign of Ram, such incident of untimely death was never heard or seen. Undoubtedly, wicked acts of Ram were causing death of children in his kingdom. Therefore, he requested that his son should be resurrected, otherwise, he would also die in front of gate of palace, then Ram would had been charged of brahman's murder.

"Residents of town and village were busy in sinful acts and measures were not taken to check it, then only, fear of untimely death was faced by citizens of kingdom." (73/17)

"Therefore it is clear that some mistake has been done by the king, then only the boy is dead. It is undoubtful." (73/18)

Ram heard sorrowful weeping of the Brahman then he became agitated. He called his ministers, Priests and brothers. His eight priests arrived there, namely Markandeya, Moudgalya, Vamdeo, Kashyap, Katyayan, Jabali, Gautam and Narad. Ram told about brahman'charge and asked for their advice, then Narada said after discussing with others, "earlier in Satyuga, only Brahmans were practicing religious traditions, other than brahmanas nobody was indulged in such practices. In Tretayug, Kshatriya has become important and is practicing religious rituals. But according to Varna Vyavastha (System of four classes) third and fourth Varnas are not permitted to practice mantras or ascetic fervor.

"Onwards, dwaparayug will come, wherein, third Varna will also be indulged in religious practice, but fourth Varna has no right to perform such religious acts in all the three yugas." (74/26)

"O king, indulging of Shudra in ascetic practice, even in Dwapar will be a crime, (while this is Tretayug). Certainly, any ill minded Shudra is practicing ascetics within your kingdom. That is why, this boy is dead. If crime or sinful acts are performed in a kingdom, that kingdom faces poverty and the king goes to hell very soon undoubtedly." (74/28,29,30)

Listening the statement of Narada, supported by every body there, Ram sent his detectives in all directions to know about unlawful acts, then a man had been found practicing fervor, hanging on a tree up side down. He was asked by Ram about his name and cast and purpose of such an act. The upward hanging person replied that his name was Shambook, a Shudra.He was practicing that act to win kingdom of deities. Hearing that, Ram cut shambook's throat by sword. during discussion on this matter, two points are to be kept in mind. Firstly, superiority and powers of Brahmans in that period and secondly, commitment of Ram towards guidelines of religious books and Brahmans, which was repeatedly told earlier. Commenting on this incident on internet, many people told Ram a cruel and insensitive towards shudras. Before commenting any thing, one must study Ramayan carefully and should mind Ram's behavior towards Nishadraj Guha, Shabari, Sugreeva, Hanuman, Angad, Jatayu etc. of backward castes. To understand the behavior of Brahmanas, let us discuss Varnashram system in short though out of topic.

When Arya arrived India, crossing Sindhu river, there was no cast system in their society. Daughters of Swayambhu Manu and then daughters of Daksha were married to sages and deities, but onwards, population of Aryan increased considerably and division and classification of society was felt necessary. Then all types of jobs were divided into four categaries i.e., (1)Mind related work, (2) Strength related works, (3)Cultivation & Trading (4)Services. Thus, four Varnas (Class) were created and were named Brahman, Kshatriya, Vaishya and Shudra. This varna system was based on work done by the person and not by birth. Nobody should feel inferior, hence every cast was declared born from the body of Brahma. Brahmana, born from head of Brahma, Kshtriya from arms, Vaishya from the belly and Shudra from lower part of body including foot etc. This division is again based on work done by the part of the body. Brain and other sensing organs like eye, ear, mouth are part of head. Thus head commands all the parts of body, aquire and distribute knowledge. Arms save the body and do other heavy works. The belly digests the food and provides strength to all body. Lower than waist, part of body is responsible for cleanliness and movement of body.

Looking to the above classification, it is clear that, Shudra was not untouchable initially and he was an important part of body of respected Brahma, without which body could not survive. Leaders of all the political parties may know the meaning of the word "Savarna" in Sanskrit and Hindi. Savarna means with or within Varna. It means Shudra is Savarna. One more thing is to be kept in mind here-initially, Varnashram system was not stiff. The purpose of this system was two fold i.e. firstly to run and organize society smoothly, secondly to develop expertise in every field of life. A man could go to another varna according to his work. for example, Vishwamitra was Kshatriya but he was a sage. Valmiki became saint from a street lifter. Many brahmanas became kings, many monks had weapons with them, like Parshuram, Agastya. Many kshatriya kings were sent to fourth varna, such as king Sudas, Kalmashpad. But because of attachment towards descendant, brahmanas changed the varnashram system from work base to birth base. Kshatriya and Vaishya also supported them for the same reason. Thus shudra remained permanently in fourth class, because they were not in a position to oppose.

In incident of slaying of Shambook, brahmanas were afraid of ascetic practice of Shambook, because if that practice continued by fourth varna then what was the means left for Brahmanas to run their lives? Moreover who would serve the society then? Therefore all priests unitedly pressurized Ram to kill Shambook, so that the trend could not spreadout. King Ram was pressurized by brahmanas and thus Shambook was slayed.

This mishappening is seven thousand years old, but same trend exists in society even today. A doctor or an advocate wants his son to become a doctor/ advocate and to take over his father's practice. In elections, candidates are selected on the basis of their caste. Nobody cares about constitution of India, which is beyond religion or caste. The person, who enjoyed the right of reservation once, again requires it for his descendants, keeping aside other backward persons of his caste. Thus, this is a natural human weakness.

Reaching old age, Ram established his and his brother's sons in separate kingdoms (Map-4).

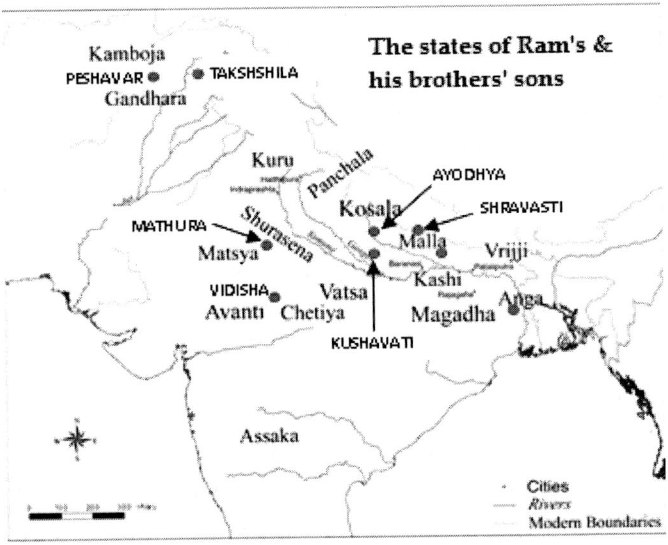

MAP NO. 04

He sent Shatrughna to conquer Mathura which was under the reign of Lawanasur, son of demon Madhu. Shatrughna returned to Ayodhya after twelve years, leaving Madhura puri, a well organized kingdom. A message from uncle Yudhajit was received by Ram, that a beautiful kingdom, called Gandharva desh is situated on the banks of river Sindhu. The Gandharvas, who are trained fighters, protect their kingdom. Ram should had invaded that kingdom. Hearing that message, Ram ordered Bharat to attack on Gandharva desh with his two sons, Taksha and Pushkala and to reign there. He enthroned Bharat as king of Gandhar kingdom, before departure. Bharat reached Kaikeya Pradesh with his army. From there, he invaded Gandhar jointly with his army and his uncle, Yudhajit's army. After many days of war, Bharat won. Bharat reorganized the Gandhara as an orderly kingdom. He settled Taksha in a newly built town, named Takshshila (Taxla in Pakistan) and Pushkal in Pushkalavati (Peshawar in Pakistan). Both the towns were progressive and prosperous. After establishing well the two capitals in five years, Bharat returned to Ayodhya, told everything to Ram. Then Ram said to Lakshman that his sons' kumar Angad and Chandraketu were wise and religious boys, they were capable to rule a kingdom. Therefore, he (Lakshman) would had selected a kingdom, where they would rule freely and fearlessly. Then, Bharat told to Ram, about Karupath pradesh. On advice of Bharat, Ram conquered that Pradesh and enthroned Angada there. He built a new capital, Angadiyapuri for Angad. Second son of Lakshman was a body builder (Malla). A separate kingdom, Malla desh was formed and its new capital Chandrakantapuri was built for Chandraketu. Ram enthroned both sons of Lakshmana on their respective kingdoms. Lakshmana stayed there upto settlement of newly formed kingdoms for one year, untill his both sons took over the control of their kingdoms. Ram divided his kingdom into two parts for his both sons. Southern part on southern bank of Saryu, called Dakshin Kosala for Kush. A new town named Kushawati, was established as its capital in Vindhya pradesh. Northern part on northern bank was called Uttara Koshala for Luv. Shrawasti was its capital. Thus Ram settled his sons as well as his brothers' sons when he became quite old.

Regarding end of life of Ram, there is a story in Uttarkand of Valmiki Ramayan. The Kala (Deity of death) came himself and requested Ram that Brahma had sent him to tell Ram, that he (Ram) have successfully done his job and his period was over. So, he might had come back to his loka, keeping aside this story, it is understood that all the four brothers died a normal death due to aging. Lakshman restricted his breathing on the bank of Saryu river. Then Ram decided to enthrone Bharat and go to forest abode. Ram said to Bharat– "arrange all the items quickly. I will enthrone you as king of Ayodhya and I will follow the path of Lakshman" (107/3). Hearing that, Bharat lost his senses, he requested Ram that he would accompany him. Ram would enthrone Kush. A message was also sent to Shatrughna at Mathura regarding their last journey. Hearing about Ram's final departure, citizen of Ayodhya gathered there. Citizen requested to Ram- "Kakutsth (Descendant of kak), if you love us, kindly permit us to follow you. We are ready to walk on Sat-path (Way of truth) with you." (107/13). Ram loved his both sons and distributed all his wealth among two sons, then sent back to their capitals.

The messenger reached Mathura. He told to Shatrughna regarding Ram's programme of final departure, death of Lakshman, enthronement of Kush, all news. He also told that Ram and Bharat both were planning to proceed to final destination, leaving Ayodhya deserted. Hearding that, Shatrughna called his sons and priests and said- "along with my brothers, I am abandoning my body. Saying thus, he enthroned his both sons on their kingdoms." (108/9) "Subahu got kingdom of Mathura and Shatrughati, that of Vidisha. Shatrughna also distributed army and wealth equally between the two sons, then he established both sons in their capitals respectively." (108/10)

Free from all responsibilities, Shatrughna departed towards Ayodhya alone by chariot. Reaching Ayodhya, Shatrughna said to Ram- "Raghunandana (Descendant of Raghu), I have come after enthroning Subahu. Therefore, I have firmly decided to follow you." (108/14)

Meanwhile, Sugreeva arrived there and said- "o Nareshwara (God of men), I have come after enthroning Angad on Kishkindha. Therefore, you assume that, I will follow you firmly." (108/23)

Ram accepted this proposal and said- "friend Sugreeva, please listen. I can not go to Deolok (Deities' abode) or Param Dham (Final abode) without you. (108/25)

Then Ram said to Vibhishana- "o demon king Vibhishan, you reside in Lanka alive, till the end of this world. He also requested to Vibhishana to continue worshiping the god Vishnu." (108/27)

Then Ram said to Hanuman- "till my stories are told and spread over in this world, you also stay happily here following my instructions." (108/33)

Thus, ordering Vibhishana and Hanumman to stay alive always, Ram permitted all others to accompany him. Next day early morning, Ram called his priest and said- "radiant fire from my agnihotra should lead with brahmanas. During journey towards ultimate destination, the decorated umbrella of my Vajpeya Yagya (A type of offering to fire) should be there over me." (109/2)

Asked by Ram, sage Vashishtha performed all desired rituals at the time of final departure. "Then Ram, wearing minimum clothes, taking Kusha (A sacred grass) in his both hands, pronouncing ved mantras (Verse from Vedas) about the existence of Paramatma (Ultimate soul), moved towards the bank of river Saryu." (109/5)

"He was not speaking any thing else except ved mantras. No other activity, except walking slowly, was visible. He had come out of his home, with all worldly desires abandoned and was moving on to the desired destination like bright sun." (109/5)

No breathing creature was left behind in Ayodhya.every body was following Ram with full faith. At a distance of approximately one and half yojan (One yojan equals to thirteen km) Ram had a view of river Saryu, flowing in western direction, then Ram along with his brothers, Sugreeva and others ,entered in water of Saryu and absorbed in profound meditation (Guptar ghat near Faizabad). Thus, a great man of initial period of Indian culture, was no more on this earth. Ayodhya was also deserted because no body alive was left there and Kusha and all his brothers went to their respective capitals.

SUMMARY

Before discussing life and character of Ram, it is interesting to go through some of the additional informations.,

Other than Religious authorities, historians and archeologists, few people, as a hobby or due to own interest, worked hard on Ramayan. According to Father Camille Bulke (Belgian Missionary), story of Ram is available in three hundred and fifty different languages of India and South East Asia. Main subject i.e. war between Ram and Rawan, is same but other descriptions are much different. Such as, in Jain Literature, Ram, Sita and Lakshman were children of first wife of king Dashrath, who were sent to forest to save them from their step mother. Due to lapse of thousands of years, difference in languages & areas such anamolies are quite natural. Therefore, Valmiki Ramayan has been taken as main base for this creation.

However, after the detail study of Valmiki Ramayan, it is clear that many incidents are incorporated later on. For example Buddha and

Tathagata words were mentioned in couple of places. Whereas, actually Valmiki Ramayan ends up with the singing of Ram's story by Kush and Luv in Namisharanya.

Many astonishing personalities and devine happenings were described in Uttarkand, which was written afterwards. However, since sage Valmiki was contemporary to Ram and Sita lived with him for twelve years, therefore Valmiki Ramayan is supposedly more authentic and closer to truth. Sage Valmiki was impelled by the life and sorrow of Sita. Earlier, seeing slaying of male of a couple of demoiselle crane and crying of female, suddenly sage Valmiki said a verse-

"O nishad (Bird catcher), you will never have peace, because you have killed one of the couple of Kraunch birds without any fault, who were engaged in love." (Balkand-2/15)

Afterwards, distressed with the sorrow of Sita, sage Valmiki created Ramayan in Anushtup Chhanda (A style of verse).

However, regarding description of divine powers and extra human powers of Ram and Rawana, it is to be remembered that poet uses similarities to the divine powers and ornamental language. To describe one's power, they impose divine powers on him and on his opponent also. It is a common practice. Here it is to remember that there are descriptions in other religions also, wherein leading character had ashtonishing and divine powers. In recent past, pope of Rome asked the list of divine acts of mother Theresa, before declaring her, a Saint. Therefore, inspite of arguing on language, one should find out the truth.

As hobby or self interest, few people have done commendable jobs, one of them is a professor from Lusiana University (U.S.A.) Subhash Kak , who in his book "ASTRONOMICAL CODE OF RIGVEDA", told that Ram was the sixtyfourth king of Ayodhya. Prior to him sixtythree kings ruled Ayodhya and the, ninty fourth was Vrihadbal or Vrihadashwa, who was killed in battle of Mahabharat by Abhimanyu.

Let us discuss another interesting point. If we consider an average period of thirty years of rule by one king, period of Vaivaswat Manu would be around two thousand years prior to Ram and period of Krishna would be around thousand years after Ram. According to calculations based on the list of descendants of Vaivaswat Manu and taking into account the period of six Manus (Vaivaswat manu was seventh), arrival of Arya in to India would be near about 8000 b.c.e. Arrival of Arya into India (First manu) was from middle east (Mesopotamia, Iraq/Iran).

Another interesting thing is a story, which has been described in puranas, as well as in Kuran Sharif and Bible. In Hindu religious books it is described that Manu(seventh) saved each type of living creatures and plants in a boat at the time of great deluge. The Manu in Puranas, is Noah in Kuran-sharif and is Nova in Bible with same story. Don't you think that Manu, Nooh and Nova are one and incident happened in Mesopotamia (Land between rivers)!!?? This is a separate subject, thus require deep study, hence stopped here.

Mr. Pushkar Bhatnagar, an I.R.S. officer with the help of Planetarium Software has calcuated planetary position described in Valmiki Ramayan & confirmed-

(1) Birth of Ram- 12:30 P.M., Chaitra Shukla Navami i.e. 10 January 5114 b.c.e.

(2) Departure for forest abode- 5 January 5089 b.c.e.

(3) Fight with Khar and Dushan- 7 October 5077 b.c.e.

(4) Hanuman in Ashoka Vatika- 12 September 5076 b.c.e.

On the basis of above findings, it may be said that Ram was around twentyfive years old when he left for forest abode. When he came back to Ayodhya and was enthroned, he was thirtynine years old. At many stages, full age of a man is said to be hundred years. While in Ramayan and other religious books, reign of Ram has been described as eleven thousand years. How is it possible? It seems that calculation is based on some other system, for period of reign or even Churayugas (Four periods- Satyuga, Treta, Dwapar and Kaliyug). A calculation system has been mentioned in Mahabharat (Van-parva, section 52), wherein, one full day (Day and night both) is taken as one year (Ahoratri Samvatsara). If period of reign of Ram is calculated on this basis, it comes to about thirty one years, but there is no solid base for such type of calculation.

One more interesting information which is available on website of National Geographic Center U.S.A. regarding Ramsetu (Adam's bridge). According to information, last ice age which was 120000 years long, ended in 16000 b.c.e. then, India and Shrilanka were connected by low lying land. Due to melting of ice sea level increased & this low land was filled with water. During 6000 b.c.e., level of water and land between India and Shrilanka was equal. Today, after 8000 years, water level is 6 to 13 feet above Ramsetu. Depth of water is not more than 13 feet any where on the bridge. Ram selected this spot for construction of bridge, after surveying sea-shore from Kodikorai to Rameshwaram in three days.

Another fact is that government of Shrilanka proposed to connect both countries by road, passing over this bridge, between Pamban and Mannar. While Indian government is interested in shipping after breaking this bridge, in the survey report of British officers in 1700 c.e. this bridge was called "Ramsetu" while after 1804 c.e. it was called "Adam's bridge". This shows that antiquity history of Indian culture was not acceptable to western historians and archeologists. Still today, the condition is same. All Indian historians and archeologists mention arrival of Arya in India in 3000-4000 b.c.e. Lord Mackale told the "Vedas", a gossip of uncouth herdsmen without considering level of the grammer and language used. Atleast now, Indians should throw out the mentality of slavery and should search the truth on their own. It should be always remembered that Indian culture and hindu religion are oldest alive culture and religion in the world.

Dr. Ramavtar Sharma` has identified 195 spots, related to Ram's journey to forest. In Chhattisgarh also, a team has surveyed the path from Ayodhya to Lanka. An overview of this journey is mentioned below:-

First step-on the banks of ganges- From Ayodhya, Ram, Sita and Lakshman departed and reached near river Tamsa at a distance of about 20 km, then after crossing river Gomati, they reached on the banks of Ganges near Shringverpur (Singraur) at a distance of about 20 km from Allahabad. At the confluence, they met with sage Bharadwaj, then crossing river Yamuna, they reached Chitrakuta on the border of M.P. and U.P. They lived here for few months, but after meeting with Bharat here, they left this place and reached to hermitage of sage Atri, near Satna (M.P.).

Second step-dandakaranya- After meeting with Atri and his wife Anusuiya, they entered into Dandakaranya and met with sage Sharbhang and sage Sutikshna as advised by sage Sutikshna,a disciple of great sage Augastya, they wandered in Dandakaranya and met several sages and hermits living on the banks of Narmada and Mahanadi rivers. During all these activities, ten years were spent in Dandakaranya. During this travel, Ram, Sita and Lakshman went to various places in Chhattisgarh, such as-Surguja, Korba, Shabrinarayan, Rajim, Konta etc. They went upto Bhadrachalam in A.P. They returned to sage Sutikshna and desired to meet his guru sage Augastya. Sage Sutikshna directed them towards south-west. Ram, Sita and Lakshman went to hermitage of sage Augastya via Ramtake (Nagpur). The hermitage was near Nasik. Sage Augastya asked Ram to stay in his hermitage, but Ram refused due to possible disturbance by demons and asked a suitable place to live and to construct their huts. Then sage Augastya suggested him, Panchwati near river Godavari. Area of Nasik is full of memories of Ram, such as– Mrigvyadheshwar, where golden dear (Marich) was killed by Ram, Sita Sarover, Ramkund, Trayambakeshwar, Jan-sthan, Sarve-Tirth (Where Jatayu was killed) and so many other places. Sarvatirth is in village takad, 56km away from Nasik.

Third step-banks of tungbhadra and kaveri- In search of Sita, after kidnapping, Ram and Lakshman met with wounded Jatayu, who was at the verge of death. Jatayu told him that Sita was taken by Rawan towards south. After funeral of Jatayu, both brothers proceeded towards south. On the way, Ram killed a demon, Kabandha, who stated that Sugreeva was well aware of southern direction. Ram should had met with Sugreeva at Rishyamook mountain. Sugreeva was also requiring help to solve his problems. Then both brothers proceeded towards south and reached Pampa Sarover, where they met with Shabari, who was Bheel by tribe and was fully devoted to religion. Shabari offered some Berry and other Roots, tasted earlier. This area is famous as surban, which is near Belgam in Karnataka and is famous for its berries.After meeting Shabari, they crossed Malaya mountain and sandal wood and reached near Rishyamook mountain, where he met Sugreeva, Hanuman etc. This place is near Hospet Railway Station with in area of Humpi in Karnataka.

Fourth step, sea shore- Ram reached with Lakshman, Sugreeva and Hanuman with Vanar Sena (Army of monkey, bear and aps) to Kodikorai on sea shore. He surveyed the sea shore for three days and then selected Rameshwaram for building a bridge to reach Lanka under the direction of Nal and Neel, who were expert in this art.

Now we will discuss the qualities and behavior of Ram,one by one-

(1) **Devotion towards guru (Teacher)-** Sage Vishwamitra was guru who taought use of various weapons. When he went to forest with sage Vishwamitra, he spent every day according to guru's will. Height of faith in guru, obeying his instructions, serving him before sleeping, every thing is visible in his devotion towards his guru. By order of sage Vishwamitra, when Ram slew tadka, Vishwamitra became pleased and imparted knowledge of new powerful weapons. During night also, till the time guru fell asleep, Ram and Lakshman kept on massaging his feet. In Janakpur also, they did not go out side without guru's permission neither Ram touched Shiva's bow. In Chitrakuta, when sage Vashishtha argues in favour of Bharat, Ram said that Bharat was very lucky, because guru was favouring him.

(2) **Devotion towards father-** Maryada purushottam (Best man among followers of limits and traditions) Ram was fully devoted towards his father. Without clear order from father, just to keep the value of his father's promise, he abandoned the throne of Ayodhya and departed to forest abode. Lakshman offered to arrest his father, mother Kaushalya also agreed but Ram refused. When Ram asked for permission to proceed to forest, king Dashrath said that Ram should had arrested him and captured the throne of Ayodhya, asRam was not bound to keep his father's promise. But due to fear of breaking of promise and defamation of his father,

Ram refused. When Kaikeyi said him about the two promises in very harsh words, he replied happily-

"I can jump into burning fire, can gulp poison, can jump into sea by order of my father." (Ayodhyakand-18/28,29)

When he asked permission from his mother to go to forest, Kaushalya –stopped him but Ram said-

"O mother, I have no power to disobey father's orders. I bow down to you, please be happy, that I am going to forest." (Ayodhyakand-21/30)

He also explained to Lakshman-

"O brother, my father is a truth speaking person, who practices and follows the path of truth. He is fearful due to deviation from truth and to face next world (After death). He should be now fearless (Because, I am going to forest)" (Ayodhyakand-22/9)

(3) Devotion towards mother- It was height of one's devotion towards mother. Ram was respectful to his mother Kaushalya as well as his step mother Kakeyi, who sent him to forest. Mother Kaushalya stopped him from going to forest, claiming that mother's order was superior to father's order, To which Ram replied that he had been ordered already to go to forest by mother Kaikeyi. In Chitrakuta, Ram met Kaikeyi first and convinced her that it was a mere misfortune, fault of time, nothing else.

Whenever Lakshman said any thing against kaikeyi, Ram checked him. At the time of departure towards forest, hundred of queens were weeping, that Ram never considered them different than Kaushlya, who would now take care off them?

(4) **Brother's love-** Ram's love towards his brothers is uncomparable. He loved his brothers very much since childhood, they were dining and sleeping altogether, they were married to four sisters. Ram felt, proposal for his enthronement alone was unjustified. Only due to his father's order and in the interest of people, he accepted it. That's why, he was happy with the demand of enthronement of Bharata. In forest, he said clearly-

"O Lakshman, I swear touching this weapon, that whatever I want i.e. religion, wealth, kingdom and all other things on this earth, is for you all." (Ayodhyakand-97/5)

During war with Meghnath, he was distressed when Lakshman was wounded. After victory of Lanka, when Vibhishana requested him to stay there, he said that he was in his own house hence no formality was required, but Bharat had been waiting for him since last fourteen years, then he had to inform Ram the best way to reach Ayodhya at the earliest. When they reached to Bhardwaj's hermitage, Ram sent Hanuman to enquire about Bharat's will. If Bharat would had been interested in kingdom, Ram would had returned back.

According to traditions, eldest son was enthroned but Ram enthroned not only his sons but his brothers'sons also in different kingdoms. Even at the end, after death of Lakshman, he entered into Saryu along with his brothers Bharat & Shatrughan.

(5) Affection towards wife- Oath of only one wife life long was a measure point in life of Ram. According to common tradition, many wives were kept by capable persons, but Ram never married twice even after abandonment of Sita. Due to wish of Sita, Ram allowed Sita to accompany him to go to forest even after many problems and kept her safe until the incident of Shurpnakha. He also educated Sita regarding History, Geography and Religion. When Sita was kidnapped, Ram wept like a common man. Lakshman had to console him many times. Regarding abandonment of Sita, when she was pregnant, one has to study the whole situation, such as king's status, status of woman in society, traditions gourning life of a woman, supremacy of brahmanas etc. After death of Rawan, Ram asked Sita for Agni-pariksha (Fire test), because Sita lived one year in Rawan's house. It was not acceptable to Ram that people defamed her afterwards. During that period, eldest son was preffered to enthrone, but he had to be supported by priests, courtiers and other noble men of state. Therfore, to satisfy every body, Agni–pariksha was essential.

While departure from Chitrakuta, Sati Ansuiya advised Sita to serve and to obey orders of her husband always. Lowest place was allowed to women in that society. Even the right of selecting her husband was a myth. In case of Sita's swayamber, it was stated that she was Virya-shulka (Award of bravery). If some body did illeagal with woman, then woman was also punished. Such as sage Gautam punished his wife and sage Parshuram slew his mother by order of his father. Very old sages and monks demanded the princesses for marriage and the kings could not deny. Ahilya, Ansuiya, every one were princesses. Story of sage Chyawan is famous, wherein he married a sixteen years old princess and invented Chyawanprash to live married life. When Bharat and Shatrughna returned from Kaikeya Pradesh, after departure of Ram to forest, then Shatrughna beat Manthara badly and Bharat checked him in the name of Ram. Bharata told Shatrughna that he was very angry with his mother Kaikeyi, he wanted to kill her, but due to fear of Ram, he could not do so. Ram never liked misbehavior with any woman. During vedic age, hermitages of famous sages were quite comfortable. Therefore, all the princes lived and studied there. The hermitages were full of milk and other food items. When Ram decided to abandon Sita, she was left near Valmiki Ashram (Valmiki's hermitage), where she was well cared and afterwards her sons, Kush and Luv became complete man with full of qualities. One more point is to be taken care that if abandonment of Sita was not according to prevailing rules of society, then why did priests not opposed? It means that living of Sita with Ram was against the tradition. Here it is mentioned that Ram did not marry again after abandonment of Sita, while in those days, it was a comman tradition, to marry more then one.

(6) Friendship- Whoso ever became friend of Ram, continued life long. He might be from any class or caste. Nishadraj Guha, Sugreeva, Hanuman are examples of this quality. The peopleout of varnashram, living in forests, were also his friends. He helped Sugreeva and Vibhishana to aquire their kingdoms. Hanuman was his very near and dear. As far as, in case of Shambook slaying, it is clear now that Ram had full faith in brahmanas and on guidelines of religious books. He lived his whole life following the rules of religion. In Dandakaranya, when Sita stopped him to kill demons because he (Ram) was a monk, Ram replied that he had vow to protect sages from demons-

"Site, I can abandon my soul, you or Lakshman also, but I can not abandon my oath to protect brahmanas." (Aranyakand-10/18)

According to this policy, he slew Shambook as per instructions of priests. When a man censures Ram for slaying of Shambook, he should remember Ram's friendship with Sugreeva, Hanuman and Guha. He always did anything on advice of brahmanas and advisors. In these days, when everybody is busy in protecting his or his relative's interest, Ram's criticism is natural.

(7) **Knowledge of weapons and books-** Ram learnt operation of various dangerous weapons from sage Vishwamitra and Augastya and acquired knowledge of religious books from sage Vashishtha. Before marriage, he performed pilgrimage all over India. Whenever time prevailed, Ram had discussed about religious books with sage Vashishtha.

(8) **Attack on south India-** Ram never attacked on south India. Actually, he went to south India after kidnapping of his wife Sita. After death of Bali and Rawan, Ram enthroned their brothers. Ram is the first man in Indian history, who had formed a country i.e. today's India. Well before Ram, when Rawan was on his expedition, he attacked north India. When he attacked Ayodhya, king Anaranya, ancestor of Ram, was killed. In Mahishmati (Maheshwar, M.P.) Rawan was fastened with rope by the king Sahastrarjuna. His grand father, sage Pulatasya came there and requested the king to release Rawan. During attack on Kailash, he was crushed by the toe of lord Shiva, that's why, he was called "Rawan". Therefore the blame on Ram, to attack south India is completelybaseless.

Ram is the greatest ancestor of all Indians beyond religion and caste. I feel very sorry, when Ram is blamed without study of his life even by the persons who don't know the names of their great grand fathers.